The Cake Stall

THE AUSTRALIAN
Women's Weekly

The Cake Stall

acp
books

CONTENTS

INTRODUCTION 6

THE LEMONADE STAND 8

GIFTS FOR MUM 12

TREATS FOR THE KIDS.................... 48

'TIS THE SEASON 82

GRANDMA'S KITCHEN 122

JAMS AND PRESERVES 160

GLOSSARY 194

CONVERSION CHART 197

INDEX............................... 198

THE CAKE STALL

A quick survey of the test kitchen reveals that although most of us spend our working lives immersed in food we all still find it pretty much impossible to walk past a cake or lolly stall or browse a local market or school fete without being tempted by the home-made offerings on display. Who can resist the allure of a perfectly pink jelly cake, a gleaming jar of marmalade, or the sweet, gritty promise of a square of fudge? What's not to love about a jar of fruit mince or a rich fruit cake at Christmas, or a tart or slice that's offered as a gift when visiting friends or family or to share with co-workers at morning tea?

Whether you want to indulge in some good old-fashioned nostalgia or you've been asked to contribute to a fundraising stall, we've devised this book so you can enjoy the fun of the fair every day with recipes for more than 120 treats that are bound to be snapped up like hot cakes.

Presentation is everything when it comes to home-made produce. If possible, present your treats in clear containers so the contents can advertise themselves. Collect interesting jars and old bottles for your jams and preserves and sterilise them according to the instructions on page 163. Hide the labels on jar lids with cloth covers, such as calico rounds tied with raffia or ribbon. Or try a double-layered lid decoration with a gingham outer and a paper doily flounce underneath.

Clear cellophane packets tied with coloured ribbon are a great way to present food. Or you can make your own inexpensively by sewing cellophane sheets together using the zigzag stitch on a sewing machine. Brown paper packages tied up with string are another good look, particularly if you have access to a pair of pinking shears to make a decorative edging and a stamping tool for a decorative motif. Chinese takeaway cardboard containers and all sorts of boxes and party favour packages are available cheaply from bargain shops and make good containers for sweets and biscuits. While you're shopping, buy a range of stickers or swing tags to attach to the fare. Attach a sample cookie, cookie cutter, or if it's Christmas, candy cane or cinnamon stick to the package. If you're supplying cakes, biscuits or slices for a stall, it's a good idea to list the ingredients on the top of the box so customers can be alerted to any components that might contain allergens. Remember that not everyone wants to buy a whole cake, so maximise sales by offering single slices and individual portions of cookies and slices.

Whatever you decide to make or bake, rest assured that the rewards for creating it will be far greater than the effort you put into making it. Home-made produce will always be appreciated for its thoughtfulness, not to mention the good old-fashioned flavour that can never be replicated in a commercial kitchen. Happy cooking.

THE LEMONADE STAND

ginger beer

$2

homemade lemonade

50°

$4

lime cordial

raspberry mint cordial

ginger beer

250g (8 ounces) fresh ginger, chopped finely
3 cups (750ml) water
2 cups (440g) caster (superfine) sugar
¼ cup (60ml) lemon juice
3 litres (12 cups) sparkling mineral water

1 Combine ginger and the water in medium
non-reactive saucepan. Bring to the boil.
Reduce heat; simmer, uncovered, 5 minutes.
Remove from heat; stand, covered, overnight
until cool.
2 Strain ginger mixture through fine sieve into
large jug. Return to same cleaned saucepan
with sugar. Stir over low heat until sugar
dissolves; bring to the boil. Reduce heat;
simmer, uncovered, without stirring, 5 minutes.
Remove from heat; stir in juice. Strain mixture
into large jug; cool. Pour into sterilised bottles;
keep refrigerated.
3 Just before serving, mix by adding four parts
sparkling mineral water to one part ginger
beer, or to taste.

prep + cook time 30 minutes (+ cooling)
makes 3 cups undiluted ginger beer syrup
or 3.75 litres diluted ginger beer
tips Use a non-reactive stainless steel, enamel
or glass saucepan for this recipe. Store ginger
beer syrup refrigerated for up to two weeks.

homemade lemonade

4 medium lemons (560g)
4 cups (880g) caster (superfine) sugar
2 cups (500ml) water
5 litres (20 cups) sparkling mineral water

1 Remove rind from lemons using a vegetable
peeler, avoiding white pith; reserve lemons.
Combine rind, sugar and the water in large
saucepan. Stir over low heat until sugar
dissolves; bring to the boil. Reduce heat; simmer,
uncovered, without stirring, about 10 minutes
or until syrup is thickened slightly; cool.
2 Squeeze juice from lemons – you will need
1 cup (250ml) lemon juice. Add juice to syrup,
strain into large jug; pour into sterilised bottles,
keep refrigerated.
3 Just before serving, mix by adding four parts
sparkling mineral water to one part lemonade,
or to taste.

prep + cook time 30 minutes (+ cooling)
makes 5 cups undiluted lemonade
or 6.25 litres diluted lemonade
tip Store lemonade syrup refrigerated
for up to two weeks.

lime cordial

3¾ cups (825g) caster (superfine) sugar
1½ cups (375ml) water
12 x 5cm (2 inch) strips lime rind
1¼ cups (310ml) lime juice, strained
4.5 litres (18 cups) still or sparkling
   mineral water

1 Combine sugar and the water in medium
saucepan; stir over low heat until sugar
dissolves. Add rind; bring to the boil. Boil,
uncovered, without stirring, 3 minutes.
Transfer hot syrup to large heatproof jug.
2 Add juice to syrup; stir until combined. Pour
syrup through fine sieve into sterilised bottles;
discard solids. Cool to room temperature.
3 Just before serving, mix by adding four parts
still or sparkling mineral water to one part lime
syrup, or to taste.

prep + cook time 25 minutes (+ cooling)
makes 4.5 cups undiluted lime syrup
or 5.6 litres diluted lime cordial
tips The lime syrup will keep in the fridge for
up to two months. Add a few drops of green
food colouring to the syrup, if you like.

raspberry mint cordial

500g frozen raspberries, thawed
3¾ cups (825g) caster (superfine) sugar
1½ cups (375ml) water
12 x 5cm (2 inch) strips lemon rind
4 sprigs fresh mint
½ cup (125ml) lemon juice
5 litres (20 cups) still or sparkling
   mineral water

1 Blend or process raspberries until smooth.
2 Combine sugar and the water in medium
saucepan; stir over low heat until sugar
dissolves. Add rind and mint; bring to the boil.
Boil, uncovered, without stirring, 3 minutes.
Transfer hot syrup to large heatproof jug; cool
10 minutes.
3 Add juice and raspberry puree to syrup;
stir until combined. Strain mixture through
muslin-lined sieve into large jug; discard
solids. Pour syrup again through fine sieve
into sterilised bottles; discard solids. Cool to
room temperature.
4 Just before serving, mix by adding four parts
still or sparkling mineral water to one part
raspberry syrup, or to taste.

prep + cook time 30 minutes (+ cooling)
makes 5 cups undiluted raspberry syrup
or 6.25 litres diluted raspberry mint cordial
tips The raspberry mint syrup will keep in
the fridge for up to one month. You could also
add fresh mint and frozen or fresh raspberries
or mixed berries to the drink, if you like.

GIFTS FOR MUM

passionfruit buttermilk cake 16

caramel nut chocolates 19

turkish delight..20

tropical toasted muesli 20

salted caramel truffles 23

chocolate marzipan almonds 23

sugar and spice almonds..25

orange and almond palmiers 25

vanilla whoopie pies 26

chocolate whoopie pies..26

almond bread 28

pistachio white chocolate brittle 28

pistachio, white chocolate and honey french macaroons......30

strawberry jelly cakes 35

raspberry cream sponge 35

buttery citrus cake 37

orange almond victoria sponge.......................................38

dundee cake 41

plum and cinnamon cake 41

hummingbird cakes 42

carrot cakes 45

chocolate and pecan torte..46

chocolate chiffon cake..47

GIFTS FOR MUM

Mothers spend so much of their lives looking after everyone else that they never seem to have time to indulge themselves. Whether it's her birthday, Christmas, Mother's Day or simply because you want her to know how special she is, here are some deliciously indulgent treats that say, "I love you, Mum" – in the sweetest possible way.

passionfruit buttermilk cake

250g (8 ounces) butter, softened
1 cup (220g) caster (superfine) sugar
3 eggs, separated
2 cups (300g) self-raising flour
¾ cup (180ml) buttermilk
¼ cup (60ml) passionfruit pulp
passionfruit icing
1½ cups (240g) icing (confectioners') sugar
¼ cup (60ml) passionfruit pulp, approximately

1 Preheat oven to 180°C/350°F. Grease and lightly flour 24cm (9½-inch) bundt tin or 20cm (8-inch) baba cake pan; tap out excess flour.
2 Beat butter and sugar in small bowl with electric mixer until light and fluffy. Beat in egg yolks, one at a time.
3 Transfer mixture to large bowl; stir in half the sifted flour and half the buttermilk, then stir in remaining flour, buttermilk and passionfruit pulp.

4 Beat egg whites in small bowl with electric mixer until soft peaks form. Fold into cake mixture, in two batches. Spread mixture into prepared tin.
5 Bake cake about 40 minutes. Stand cake in pan 5 minutes before turning onto wire rack to cool.
6 Meanwhile, make passionfruit icing.
7 Drizzle passionfruit icing over cold cake.
passionfruit icing Sift icing sugar into medium heatproof bowl; stir in enough passionfruit pulp to form a thick paste. Stand bowl over small saucepan of simmering water; stir until icing is of a pouring consistency (do not overheat).

prep + cook time 1 hour (+ cooling) **serves** 8

Cake is best made on the day of serving. Un-iced cake suitable to freeze for up to three months.

passionfruit
buttermilk cake

caramel nut chocolates

caramel nut chocolates

60g (2 ounces) butter
½ cup (110g) caster (superfine) sugar
1 tablespoon golden syrup or treacle
¾ cup (250g) sweetened condensed milk
½ teaspoon vanilla extract
½ cup (75g) unsalted peanuts,
   chopped coarsely
¼ cup (25g) ground hazelnuts or almonds
100g (3 ounces) dark eating (semi-sweet)
   chocolate, chopped coarsely
1 teaspoon vegetable oil
50g (1½ ounces) dark eating (semi-sweet)
   chocolate, extra, melted

1 Combine butter, sugar and syrup in small
saucepan; stir over low heat until sugar
dissolves. Stir in condensed milk; bring to
the boil. Reduce heat; cook, stirring, about
6 minutes or until mixture turns a caramel
colour. Remove from heat; stir in extract and
nuts. Transfer mixture to medium heatproof
bowl; cool 10 minutes.
2 Roll rounded teaspoons of mixture into
balls; place on tray. Refrigerate until firm.
3 Combine chocolate and oil in medium
heatproof bowl; stir over medium saucepan
of simmering water until smooth. Dip balls
in chocolate mixture using a fork or skewer. Lift
balls from chocolate; allow excess chocolate to
drip away. Place on tray lined with aluminium
foil or baking paper. Refrigerate until set.
4 Drizzle extra melted chocolate over balls.
Refrigerate until set.

prep + cook time 55 minutes
(+ refrigeration & cooling) **makes** 32
tip Refrigerate in an airtight container
for up to one week.

turkish delight

¼ cup (45g) gelatine
¼ cup (60ml) water
3 cups (660g) caster (superfine) sugar
2 cups (500ml) water, extra
¾ cup (110g) wheaten cornflour (cornstarch)
2 tablespoons glucose syrup
¼ cup (60ml) rosewater
red food colouring
⅔ cup (110g) icing (confectioners') sugar

1 Grease deep 19cm (7¾-inch) square cake pan.
2 Sprinkle gelatine over the water in small jug; stand jug in small saucepan of simmering water. Stir until gelatine dissolves.
3 Combine caster sugar and ¾ cup of the extra water in medium saucepan; stir over low heat until sugar dissolves. Bring to the boil; boil, without stirring, until temperature of the syrup reaches 116°C/235°F (soft ball) on candy thermometer. Simmer at 116°C/235°F for 5 minutes, without stirring, regulating heat to maintain temperature at 116°C/235°F. Remove pan from heat.
4 Meanwhile, place cornflour in another medium saucepan; gradually blend in the remaining extra water. Bring to the boil, stirring, until mixture thickens.
5 Gradually stir hot sugar syrup, gelatine mixture and glucose into cornflour mixture; bring to the boil, stirring. Reduce heat; simmer, stirring, about 10 minutes or until mixture thickens a little more. Remove pan from heat; whisk in rosewater, tint with red food colouring.
6 Strain mixture through fine sieve into cake pan; skim any scum from surface. Stand 15 minutes; cover surface with lightly greased baking paper, stand overnight.
7 Turn turkish delight onto board dusted with sifted icing sugar, dust with more sifted icing sugar; cut with icing-sugar-coated knife. Roll pieces in remaining sifted icing sugar.

prep + cook time 40 minutes (+ cooling & standing) makes 48
tips You must use a candy thermometer to get the correct consistency for turkish delight. Store turkish delight in an airtight container at room temperature for up to two weeks.

tropical toasted muesli

½ cup (180g) honey
½ cup (110g) firmly packed light brown sugar
¼ cup (60ml) rice bran oil
3 cups (270g) rolled oats
1¼ cups (100g) desiccated coconut
1 cup (140g) macadamia nuts, chopped coarsely
1 cup (150g) sunflower seed kernels
2 teaspoons ground cinnamon
1 teaspoon ground ginger
1 cup (50g) flaked coconut
½ cup (90g) coarsely chopped dried pineapple
½ cup (65g) coarsely chopped dried mango
⅓ cup (60g) coarsely chopped dried papaya

1 Preheat the oven to 180°C/350°F. Line two large oven trays with baking paper.
2 Combine honey, sugar and oil in small saucepan; stir over low heat until sugar dissolves.
3 Combine oats, desiccated coconut, nuts, seeds and spices in large bowl; stir in warm honey mixture until well combined. Divide mixture between oven trays and spread evenly. Bake, stirring halfway through cooking, for about 30 minutes or until golden and crisp. Cool on trays.
4 Combine toasted oat mixture, flaked coconut and dried fruits in large bowl.

prep + cook time 50 minutes (+ cooling)
makes 12 cups (24 serves)
tip Store in an airtight container in refrigerator for up to one month.

turkish delight

tropical toasted muesli

salted caramel truffles

salted caramel truffles

⅓ cup (75g) caster (superfine) sugar
2 tablespoons water
⅔ cup (160ml) pouring cream
200g (6½ ounces) dark eating (semi-sweet)
  chocolate, chopped coarsely
1 teaspoon sea salt flakes
200g (6½ ounces) milk eating chocolate, melted

1 Combine sugar and the water in small
saucepan; stir over heat, without boiling,
until sugar dissolves. Bring to the boil; boil,
uncovered, without stirring, until golden
brown. Add cream; stir over low heat until
toffee pieces melt. Remove from heat; stir in
dark chocolate and half the salt until smooth.
Refrigerate mixture overnight.
2 Working with a quarter of the chocolate
mixture at a time (keep remainder
refrigerated), roll rounded teaspoons of
mixture into balls; place on foil-lined tray.
Freeze until firm.
3 Working quickly, using two forks, dip
truffles in milk chocolate. Return truffles to
tray; sprinkle with remaining salt. Refrigerate
truffles until firm.

prep + cook time 40 minutes (+ refrigeration
& freezing) **makes** 25

chocolate marzipan almonds

30 (40g) whole blanched almonds
200g (6½ ounces) marzipan or almond paste
125g (4 ounces) dark eating (semi-sweet)
  chocolate, melted

1 Preheat oven to 180°C/350°F.
2 Roast nuts in single layer on oven tray about
5 minutes or until browned lightly; cool.
3 Mould level teaspoons of paste around each nut.
Place on wire rack; stand, uncovered, overnight,
until dry to touch.
4 Using two forks, dip each nut into chocolate.
Place nuts on foil-lined tray; leave to set at room
temperature.

prep + cook time 40 minutes (+ standing) **makes** 30

orange and
almond palmiers

sugar and spice almonds

orange and almond palmiers

1 cup (150g) vienna almonds
15g (½ ounce) butter
2 tablespoons orange-flavoured liqueur
2 teaspoons finely grated orange rind
2 tablespoons demerara (light brown) sugar
2 sheets butter puff pastry
1 egg, beaten lightly
orange glacé icing
1 cup (160g) icing (confectioners') sugar
15g (½ ounce) butter
½ teaspoon finely grated orange rind
2 teaspoons orange juice
2 teaspoons hot water, approximately

1 Blend or process nuts, butter, liqueur and rind to a coarse paste.
2 Sprinkle board with half the sugar; place one sheet of pastry on the sugar. Roll pastry gently into sugar. Spread half the nut mixture over pastry; fold two opposite sides of pastry inwards to meet in the middle. Flatten folded pastry slightly; brush with a little egg. Fold each side in half to meet in the middle; flatten slightly. Fold the two sides in half again, so they touch in the middle. Repeat process with remaining sugar, pastry, nut mixture and egg. Cover pastry rolls; refrigerate 30 minutes.
3 Preheat oven to 200°C/400°F. Grease two oven trays.
4 Cut pastry rolls into 1cm (½-inch) slices; place slices about 2.5cm (1 inch) apart on trays.
5 Bake palmiers about 12 minutes. Transfer to wire racks to cool.

6 Meanwhile, make orange glacé icing.
7 Spread one side of palmiers with icing; set at room temperature.
orange glacé icing Sift icing sugar into small heatproof bowl; stir in butter, rind, juice and enough of the water to make a thick paste. Place bowl over small saucepan of simmering water; stir until icing is spreadable.

prep + cook time 45 minutes (+ refrigeration)
makes 32

sugar and spice almonds

1½ cups (240g) pure icing (confectioners') sugar
1½ tablespoons ground cinnamon
5 cups (750g) almond kernels

1 Preheat oven to 180°C/350°F. Line large baking dish with baking paper.
2 Sift icing sugar and cinnamon together twice into medium bowl.
3 Place nuts in colander; rinse under cold water. Tip wet nuts into baking dish. Sift the cinnamon mixture over nuts; toss to coat.
4 Roast almonds about 20 minutes, stirring halfway through cooking, or until fragrant and browned. Cool in dish; they will become crisp on cooling. Separate almonds and store in airtight jars or package in cellophane bags.

prep + cook time 30 minutes (+ cooling)
makes 5 cups
tip Nuts will keep in an airtight container or in sealed bags in a cool, dry spot for up to one month.

Whoopie pies are a cross between a soft biscuit and a cake. They are also known as hucklebucks, gobs and BFOs (big fat Oreos). Store filled pies in an airtight container in the refrigerator for up to three days.

vanilla whoopie pies

125g (4 ounces) unsalted butter, softened
2 teaspoons vanilla extract
½ cup (110g) caster (superfine) sugar
1 egg
1¼ cups (185g) plain (all-purpose) flour
¼ cup (35g) self-raising flour
1 teaspoon bicarbonate of soda (baking soda)
⅔ cup (160ml) buttermilk
butter cream filling
60g (2 ounces) unsalted butter, softened
¾ cup (120g) icing (confectioners') sugar
1 tablespoon milk

1 Preheat oven to 200°C/400°F. Grease and line oven trays with baking paper.
2 Beat butter, extract, sugar and egg in small bowl with electric mixer until light and fluffy.
3 Beat in sifted dry ingredients and buttermilk in two batches, on low speed, until mixture is smooth.
4 Drop level tablespoons of mixture onto trays, 4cm (1½ inches) apart. Bake about 8 minutes. Cool on trays.
5 Meanwhile, make butter cream filling. Join cooled pies with butter cream filling.
butter cream filling Beat butter in small bowl with electric mixer until as white as possible. Gradually beat in half the sifted icing sugar and the milk; beat in remaining sifted icing sugar.

prep + cook time 25 minutes (+ cooling)
makes 16

chocolate whoopie pies

125g (4 ounces) unsalted butter, softened
2 teaspoons vanilla extract
½ cup (110g) firmly packed light brown sugar
1 egg
¾ cup (75g) plain (all-purpose) flour
¼ cup (35g) self-raising flour
1 teaspoon bicarbonate of soda (baking soda)
⅓ cup (35g) cocoa powder
⅔ cup (160ml) buttermilk
butter cream filling
60g (2 ounces) unsalted butter, softened
¾ cup (120g) icing (confectioners') sugar
1 tablespoon milk

1 Preheat oven to 200°C/400°F. Grease and line oven trays with baking paper.
2 Beat butter, extract, sugar and egg in small bowl with electric mixer until light and fluffy.
3 Beat in sifted dry ingredients and buttermilk, in two batches, on low speed, until mixture is smooth.
4 Drop level tablespoons of mixture onto trays, 4cm (1½ inches) apart. Bake about 8 minutes. Cool on trays.
5 Meanwhile, make butter cream filling. Join cooled pies with butter cream filling.
butter cream filling Beat butter in small bowl with electric mixer until as white as possible. Gradually beat in half the sifted icing sugar and the milk; beat in remaining sifted icing sugar.

prep + cook time 25 minutes (+ cooling)
makes 16

chocolate whoopie pies

vanilla whoopie pies

Almond bread is an excellent accompaniment to desserts such as mousse, sorbet and ice-cream. It will keep for months if stored in an airtight container at room temperature.

almond bread

3 egg whites
½ cup (110g) caster (superfine) sugar
1 cup (150g) plain (all-purpose) flour
¾ cup (120g) almond kernels

1 Preheat oven to 180°C/350°F. Grease 10cm x 20cm (4-inch x 8-inch) loaf pan.
2 Beat egg whites in small bowl with electric mixer until soft peaks form. Gradually add sugar, beating until dissolved between additions.
3 Fold sifted flour and nuts into egg white mixture; spread mixture into pan. Bake about 30 minutes. Cool bread in pan. Remove bread from pan, wrap in foil; stand overnight.
4 Preheat oven to 150°C/300°F.
5 Using a sharp serrated knife, cut the bread into wafer-thin slices. Place slices, in single layer, on ungreased oven trays. Bake about 45 minutes or until dry and crisp.

prep + cook time 1 hour 35 minutes
(+ cooling & standing) makes 40 slices

pistachio white chocolate brittle

2 cups (440g) caster (superfine) sugar
½ cup (125ml) water
2 tablespoons rosewater
1 cup (140g) unsalted, roasted, shelled pistachios, chopped coarsely
1 tablespoon dried rose petals
90g (3 ounces) white eating chocolate, melted

1 Line oven tray with baking paper.
2 Stir sugar and the water in medium saucepan over heat, without boiling, until sugar dissolves. Stir in rosewater; bring to the boil. Boil, uncovered, without stirring, until golden brown. Allow bubbles to subside; add nuts. Pour mixture onto tray; sprinkle with rose petals. Leave to set at room temperature.
3 Turn toffee over; spread chocolate over flat side of brittle. Leave to set at room temperature. Break brittle into pieces.

prep + cook time 25 minutes (+ standing)
serves 16
tip Dried rose petals are available from specialist food stores.

almond bread

pistachio white
chocolate brittle

pistachio, white chocolate and honey french macaroons

⅓ cup (45g) unsalted, roasted,
  shelled pistachios
3 egg whites
¼ cup (55g) caster (superfine) sugar
green food colouring
1¼ cups (200g) icing (confectioners') sugar
¾ cup (90g) ground almonds
honeyed white chocolate ganache
¼ cup (60ml) pouring cream
155g (5 ounces) white eating chocolate,
  chopped coarsely
2 teaspoons honey

1 Preheat oven to 150°C/300°F. Grease oven
trays; line with baking paper.
2 Process nuts until finely ground.
3 Beat egg whites in small bowl with electric
mixer until soft peaks form. Add caster sugar
and a few drops of green food colouring; beat
until sugar dissolves. Transfer mixture to large
bowl. Fold in ¼ cup of the ground pistachios,
sifted icing sugar and ground almonds, in
two batches.

4 Spoon mixture into piping bag fitted with
1cm (½-inch) plain tube. Pipe 4cm (1½-inch)
rounds about 2.5cm (1 inch) apart onto trays.
Tap trays on bench so macaroons spread
slightly. Sprinkle macaroons with remaining
ground pistachios; stand 30 minutes.
5 Bake macaroons about 20 minutes. Cool
on trays.
6 Meanwhile, make honeyed white
chocolate ganache.
7 Sandwich macaroons with ganache.
honeyed white chocolate ganache Bring cream
to the boil in small saucepan. Remove from
heat; pour over chocolate and honey in small
heatproof bowl, stir until smooth. Stand at
room temperature until spreadable.

prep + cook time 45 minutes (+ standing)
makes 16

pistachio, white chocolate and honey french macaroons

strawberry jelly cakes

raspberry cream sponge

strawberry jelly cakes

6 eggs
⅔ cup (150g) caster (superfine) sugar
⅓ cup (50g) cornflour (cornstarch)
½ cup (75g) plain (all-purpose) flour
⅓ cup (50g) self-raising flour
80g (2½ ounces) strawberry jelly crystals
2 cups (160g) desiccated coconut
1 cup (250ml) thickened (heavy)
  cream, whipped

1 Preheat oven to 180°C/350°F. Grease
20cm x 30cm (8-inch x 12-inch) rectangular
pan; line base and long sides with baking paper,
extending paper 5cm (2 inches) over sides.
2 Beat eggs in large bowl with electric mixer
about 10 minutes or until thick and creamy;
gradually add sugar, beating until dissolved
between additions. Triple-sift flours; fold into
egg mixture.
3 Spread mixture into pan; bake about
35 minutes. Turn cake immediately onto
baking-paper-covered wire rack to cool.
4 Meanwhile, make jelly as per packet
instructions; refrigerate until set to the
consistency of unbeaten egg white.
5 Trim all sides of cake. Cut cake into
15 squares; dip squares into jelly, drain
off excess. Place coconut into medium
bowl; toss squares in coconut. Refrigerate
30 minutes. Halve cakes horizontally;
sandwich cakes with whipped cream.

prep + cook time 50 minutes (+ refrigeration)
makes 15

raspberry cream sponge

4 eggs
¾ cup (165g) caster (superfine) sugar
⅔ cup (100g) wheaten cornflour (cornstarch)
¼ cup (30g) custard powder
1 teaspoon cream of tartar
½ teaspoon bicarbonate of soda (baking soda)
¾ cup (240g) raspberry jam
1½ cups (375ml) thickened (heavy) cream, whipped
raspberry glacé icing
45g (1½ ounces) fresh raspberries
2 cups (320g) icing (confectioners') sugar
15g (½ ounce) butter, softened
2 teaspoons hot water, approximately

1 Preheat oven to 180°C/350°F. Grease deep 22cm
(9-inch) square cake pan with butter.
2 Beat eggs and sugar in small bowl with electric
mixer about 10 minutes or until thick and creamy
and sugar has dissolved; transfer to large bowl.
3 Sift dry ingredients twice, then sift over egg
mixture; fold dry ingredients into egg mixture.
Spread mixture into pan.
4 Bake sponge about 25 minutes. Turn sponge
immediately onto baking-paper-covered wire rack,
then turn top-side up to cool.
5 Meanwhile, make raspberry glacé icing.
6 Halve sponge horizontally; sandwich with jam
and cream. Spread sponge with icing; sprinkle
with fresh rose petals.
raspberry glacé icing Push raspberries through fine
sieve into small heatproof bowl; discard solids. Sift
icing sugar into same bowl; stir in butter and enough
of the water to make a thick paste. Place bowl over
small saucepan of simmering water; stir until icing
is spreadable.

prep + cook time 50 minutes (+ cooling) **serves** 16
tip Use a serrated or electric knife to split and cut
the sponge.

buttery citrus cake

buttery citrus cake

250g (8 ounces) butter, softened
1 tablespoon each finely grated orange
   and lemon rind
1½ cups (330g) caster (superfine) sugar
4 eggs
1½ cups (225g) self-raising flour
½ cup (75g) plain (all-purpose) flour
½ cup (125ml) orange juice
¼ cup (60ml) lemon juice
candied citrus slices
1 cup (220g) caster (superfine) sugar
½ cup (125ml) water
1 medium orange (240g), sliced thinly
1 medium lime (75g), sliced thinly
glacé icing
2 cups (320g) icing (confectioners') sugar
¼ cup (60ml) boiling water

1 Preheat oven to 160°C/325°F. Grease deep 22cm (9-inch) round cake pan; line base and side with baking paper.
2 Beat butter, rinds and sugar in large bowl with electric mixer until light and fluffy. Beat in eggs, one at a time. Fold in sifted flours and juices, in two batches; spread mixture into pan.
3 Bake cake about 1 hour 10 minutes. Stand cake in pan 10 minutes before turning, top-side up, onto wire rack to cool.
4 Meanwhile, make candied citrus slices. Make glacé icing.
5 Drizzle cake with glacé icing. Just before serving, top with candied citrus slices.
candied citrus slices Combine sugar and the water in large frying pan. Stir over low heat, without boiling, until sugar dissolves; add orange and lime slices. Bring to the boil. Reduce heat to low; simmer, uncovered, 15 minutes, turning slices occasionally. Remove from heat; cool slices on wire rack.
glacé icing Sift icing sugar into medium heatproof bowl; add the boiling water, stir until smooth.

prep + cook time 1 hour 45 minutes **serves** 8
tips This recipe can be made four days ahead; store in an airtight container at room temperature. You will need about two oranges and one lemon for the cake. Un-iced cake is suitable to freeze.

orange almond victoria sponge

185g (6 ounces) unsalted butter, softened
1 teaspoon vanilla extract
¾ cup (165g) caster (superfine) sugar
3 eggs
¼ cup (60ml) milk
1½ cups (225g) self-raising flour
1 cup (320g) orange marmalade, warmed
1¼ cups (310ml) thickened (heavy) cream
2 tablespoons icing (confectioners') sugar
½ cup (40g) flaked almonds, roasted

1 Preheat oven to 180°C/350°F. Grease deep 20cm (8 inch) ring pan well with butter.
2 Beat butter, extract and caster sugar in small bowl with electric mixer until light and fluffy. Beat in eggs, one at a time. Stir in milk and sifted flour, in two batches.
3 Spread mixture into pan; bake about 30 minutes. Turn sponge immediately onto baking-paper-covered wire rack; turn top-side up to cool.
4 Meanwhile, strain marmalade through fine sieve; reserve syrup and rind separately.
5 Beat cream and half the icing sugar in small bowl with electric mixer until soft peaks form.
6 Split sponge into three layers. Place one layer onto serving plate, cut-side up; spread with half the marmalade syrup. Top with another layer of sponge and remaining syrup; top with remaining layer of sponge. Cut sponge into 12 pieces, keeping cake in ring shape.
7 Spread two-thirds of the cream around side of sponge; press almonds into cream. Spoon remaining cream into piping bag fitted with 1cm (½-inch) fluted tube. Pipe rosettes on top of cake; top with some of the reserved rind. Serve sponge dusted with remaining sifted icing sugar.

prep + cook time 55 minutes (+ cooling)
serves 12
tip It is fine to use just 1 x 300ml carton of cream in this recipe.

orange almond
victoria sponge

dundee cake

plum and
cinnamon cake

dundee cake

180g (5½ ounces) butter, softened
¾ cup (165g) caster (superfine) sugar
5 eggs, beaten lightly
1½ cups (225g) plain (all-purpose) flour
½ cup (75g) self-raising flour
½ teaspoon mixed spice
⅓ cup (80ml) milk
1¼ cups (200g) raisins, chopped coarsely
1½ cups (250g) currants
1¼ cups (200g) sultanas
⅓ cup (70g) red glacé cherries,
   chopped coarsely
2 tablespoons mixed peel
½ cup (80g) blanched almonds
1 tablespoon brandy

1 Preheat oven to 150°C/300°F. Line deep
19cm (7½-inch) square cake pan with
three layers of baking paper, extending
paper 5cm (2 inches) above edges.
2 Beat butter, sugar, eggs, sifted dry ingredients
and milk in large bowl with electric mixer
on medium speed about 3 minutes or until
mixture becomes pale in colour. Stir in
fruit and half the nuts.
3 Spread mixture into pan; decorate top with
remaining nuts. Bake about 2 hours. Brush
hot cake with brandy; cover tightly with foil.
Cool in pan.

prep + cook time 3 hours 20 minutes (+ cooling)
serves 16

plum and cinnamon cake

½ cup (125g) reduced-fat dairy-free spread
1 teaspoon vanilla extract
½ cup (100g) firmly packed light brown sugar
3 eggs, separated
½ cup (75g) self-raising flour
½ cup (80g) wholemeal self-raising flour
1 teaspoon ground cinnamon
4 whole canned plums in syrup, drained,
   halved, seeded
2 teaspoons icing (confectioners') sugar

1 Preheat oven to moderate 180°C/350°F.
Grease deep 20cm (8-inch) ring pan; line base
with baking paper.
2 Beat spread, extract, sugar and egg yolks in
small bowl with electric mixer until light
and fluffy. Transfer mixture to medium bowl;
stir in sifted flours and cinnamon.
3 Beat egg whites in small bowl with electric
mixer until soft peaks form; fold into flour
mixture, in two batches.
4 Spread mixture into pan; place plums,
cut-side down, on top of mixture. Bake about
30 minutes. Stand cake in pan 10 minutes before
turning, top-side up, onto wire rack to cool.
5 Serve dusted with sifted icing sugar.

prep + cook time 45 minutes serves 12

hummingbird cakes

1 cup (150g) plain (all-purpose) flour
½ cup (75g) self-raising flour
½ teaspoon bicarbonate of soda (baking soda)
½ teaspoon each ground cinnamon and ground ginger
1 cup (220g) firmly packed light brown sugar
½ cup (45g) desiccated coconut
440g (14 ounces) canned crushed pineapple, drained well
1 cup mashed banana
2 eggs, beaten lightly
¾ cup (180ml) vegetable oil
½ cup (50g) roasted walnut halves
lemon icing
1 cup (160g) icing (confectioners') sugar
10g (½ ounce) butter, melted
1½ tablespoons lemon juice, approximately

1 Preheat oven to 180°C/350°F. Grease three 8cm x 16cm (3-inch x 6-inch) loaf pans; line bases and long sides with baking paper.
2 Sift flours, soda, spices and sugar into large bowl. Stir in the coconut, pineapple, banana, eggs and oil until combined.
3 Divide mixture among prepared pans; place on oven tray. Bake about 45 minutes. Cool cakes in containers on wire rack.
4 Meanwhile make lemon icing.
5 Drizzle icing over cakes and decorate with walnuts.
lemon icing Sift icing sugar into small heatproof bowl. Stir in butter and enough of the juice to make a thick paste. Place over small saucepan of simmering water; stir until icing is a pourable consistency.

prep and cook time 1 hour **makes** 3 cakes (each cake serves 6)
tips You will need two large (about 230g each) overripe bananas.
You could use rectangular foil storage containers (8cm x 16cm, base measurement, 2-cup (500ml) capacity) to bake these cakes. The containers are available from most supermarkets.

hummingbird cakes

carrot cakes

carrot cakes

⅓ cup (80ml) vegetable oil
½ cup (110g) firmly packed light brown sugar
1 egg
1 cup firmly packed, coarsely grated carrot
⅓ cup (40g) finely chopped walnuts
¾ cup (110g) self-raising flour
½ teaspoon mixed spice
1 tablespoon pepitas, chopped finely
1 tablespoon finely chopped dried apricots
1 tablespoon finely chopped walnuts, extra
lemon cream cheese frosting
90g (3 ounces) cream cheese, softened
30g (1 ounce) unsalted butter, softened
1 teaspoon finely grated lemon rind
1½ cups (240g) icing (confectioners') sugar

1 Preheat oven to 180°C/350°F. Line 18 holes
of two 12-hole (2-tablespoon/40ml) deep
flat-based patty pans with paper cases.
2 Beat oil, sugar and egg in small bowl with
electric mixer until thick and creamy. Stir
in carrot and nuts, then sifted flour and
spice. Divide mixture among paper cases.
3 Bake cakes about 20 minutes. Stand cakes
5 minutes before turning top-side up onto
wire rack to cool.
4 Meanwhile, make lemon cream cheese
frosting.
5 Spoon lemon cream cheese frosting into
piping bag fitted with 2cm (¾-inch) fluted tube;
pipe frosting onto cakes. Sprinkle cakes with
combined pepitas, apricots and extra nuts.
lemon cream cheese frosting Beat cream
cheese, butter and rind in small bowl with
electric mixer until light and fluffy; gradually
beat in sifted icing sugar.

prep + cook time 45 minutes (+ cooling)
makes 18

chocolate and pecan torte

200g (6½ ounces) dark eating (semi-sweet)
  chocolate, chopped coarsely
150g (4½ ounces) butter, chopped coarsely
5 eggs, separated
¾ cup (165g) caster (superfine) sugar
1½ cups (150g) ground pecans
ganache
½ cup (125ml) pouring cream
200g (6½ ounces) dark eating (semi-sweet)
  chocolate, chopped coarsely

1 Preheat oven to 180°C/350°F. Grease deep
22cm (9-inch) round cake pan; line base and
side with baking paper.
2 Stir chocolate and butter in small saucepan
over low heat until smooth; cool 10 minutes.
3 Beat egg yolks and sugar in small bowl with
electric mixer until thick and creamy. Transfer
to large bowl; fold in chocolate mixture and
ground pecans.

4 Beat egg whites in small bowl with electric
mixer until soft peaks form; fold into chocolate
mixture, in two batches. Pour mixture into
pan; bake about 55 minutes. Stand cake
15 minutes; turn, top-side up, onto baking-
paper-covered wire rack to cool.
5 Meanwhile, make ganache.
6 Pour ganache over cake; refrigerate cake
30 minutes before serving.
ganache Bring cream to the boil in small
saucepan. Remove from heat; add chocolate,
stir until smooth.

prep + cook time 1 hour 20 minutes (+ standing
& refrigeration) **serves** 8

If you can't find ground pecans,
simply blend or process 150g
(4½ ounces) of roasted pecans until
they are finely ground. Be sure to
use the pulse button, however,
because you want to achieve a
flour-like texture, not a paste.

chocolate and
pecan torte

chocolate chiffon cake

½ cup (50g) cocoa powder
¾ cup (180ml) boiling water
2 cups (300g) self-raising flour
1½ cups (330g) caster (superfine) sugar
7 eggs, separated
½ cup (125ml) vegetable oil
1 teaspoon vanilla extract
walnut praline
1 cup (220g) caster (superfine) sugar
½ cup (50g) walnuts
60g (2 ounces) dark eating (semi-sweet)
   chocolate, chopped coarsely
brandied butter cream
190g (6 ounces) butter, softened
3 cups (480g) icing (confectioners') sugar
¼ cup (25g) cocoa powder
¼ cup (60ml) brandy

chocolate chiffon cake

1 Preheat oven to 180°C/350°F. Grease deep 22cm (9 inch) round cake pan; line base and side with baking (parchment) paper.
2 Blend cocoa with the water in small bowl; cool. Sift flour and sugar into large bowl; add cocoa mixture, egg yolks, oil and extract. Beat with electric mixer until smooth and mixture has changed to a paler colour.
3 Beat egg whites in large bowl with electric mixer until soft peaks form; fold into cocoa mixture, in four batches.
4 Pour mixture into pan; bake about 1 hour. Stand cake 5 minutes before turning, top-side up, onto wire rack to cool.
5 Meanwhile, make walnut praline; make brandied butter cream.
6 Split cold cake into three layers; sandwich layers with some of the butter cream. Spread cake evenly with remaining butter cream; decorate with walnut praline.

walnut praline Place sugar in heavy-based frying pan; cook over heat, without stirring, until sugar is melted and golden brown. Add nuts; pour onto greased oven tray. Cool. Blend or process praline with chocolate until finely chopped.
brandied butter cream Beat butter in small bowl with electric mixer until as white as possible. Beat in sifted icing sugar and cocoa, then brandy.

prep + cook time 1 hour 30 minutes **serves** 16

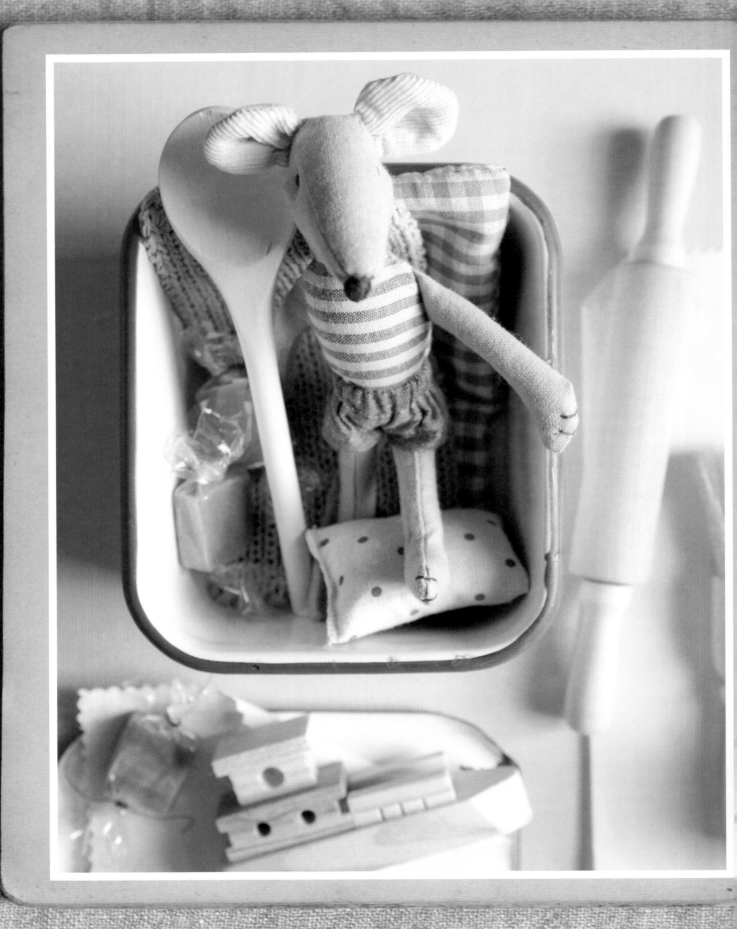

TREATS FOR THE KIDS

toffees 54
toffee apples 54
honey joys 56
candied popcorn 56
cupcakes 58
toffee-on-a-stick 60
fudge-frosted chocolate cupcakes 60
chewy chocolate slice 63
crunchy bubble bars 63
coconut ice 64
marshmallow treats 64
gingerbread men 67
chunky chewy choc-chip cookies 68
chocolate fudge 70
chocolate raspberry brownies 71
choc-vanilla noughts & crosses 72
patty cakes with glacé icing 73
coconut ice cakes 74
creamy caramels 74
chocolate coconut rough slice 76
banana cupcakes with maple cream frosting 76
chocolate freckle slice 79
peanut butter cookies 79
apricot choc-chip muesli bars 81
passionfruit marshmallows 81

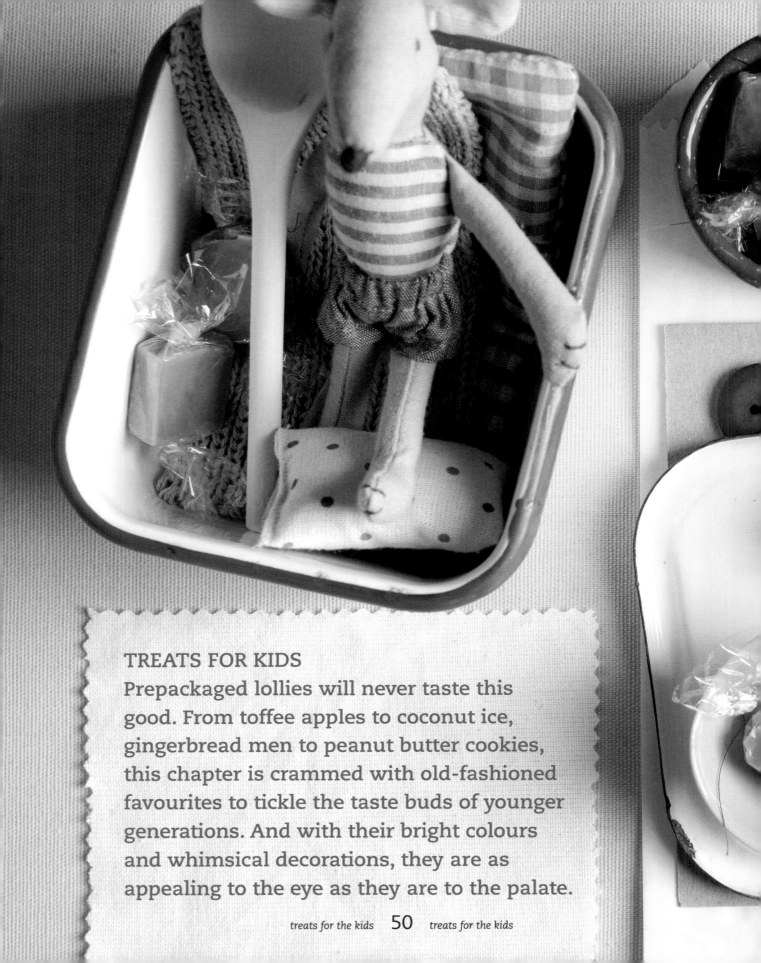

TREATS FOR KIDS

Prepackaged lollies will never taste this good. From toffee apples to coconut ice, gingerbread men to peanut butter cookies, this chapter is crammed with old-fashioned favourites to tickle the taste buds of younger generations. And with their bright colours and whimsical decorations, they are as appealing to the eye as they are to the palate.

toffees (p 54)

toffees

3 cups (660g) caster (superfine) sugar
1 cup (250ml) water
¼ cup (60ml) brown vinegar
cachous or hundreds and thousands

1 Line 12-hole (2-tablespoon/40ml) deep flat-based patty pan with paper cases.
2 Combine sugar, the water and vinegar in medium heavy-based saucepan; stir over low heat until sugar dissolves. Bring to the boil; boil, uncovered, without stirring, about 15 minutes or until temperature reaches 160°C/325°F on candy thermometer.
3 Remove from heat; allow bubbles to subside. Pour toffee into paper cases. Stand toffees about 3 minutes before decorating with hundreds and thousands or cachous. Stand at room temperature until set.

prep + cook time 30 minutes (+ standing)
makes 12
tips For easy pouring, use a saucepan with a pouring lip or carefully transfer the hot toffee to a heatproof jug.
If you do not have a candy thermometer, the syrup is ready when golden in colour and when a little of the syrup is dropped into a glass of cold water and becomes brittle immediately. Boiling the toffee to this stage will give you a good hard toffee.
If you prefer the "stick-jaw" or more stretchy toffee, boil for about 10 minutes only (130°C/260°F on candy thermometer) or until a small amount, when dropped into cold water, forms a hard ball between the fingers.
Toffees can be made up to four days ahead. Store in an airtight container interleaved with baking paper or foil in a cool dry place.

toffee apples

12 small red or green apples (1.5kg)
12 x 20cm (8-inch) long wooden sticks, available from craft shops
4 cups (880g) caster (superfine) sugar
1 cup (250ml) water
⅓ cup (80ml) glucose syrup
red or green food colouring

1 Line two baking trays with baking paper.
2 Wash apples under cold water; stand on wire rack until completely dry (do not rub apples with a cloth). Push a wooden stick three-quarters of the way through each apple from stem end.
3 Combine sugar, the water, glucose and colouring in large saucepan; stir over low heat until sugar dissolves. Bring to the boil; boil, uncovered, about 10 minutes or until mixture reaches 154°C/300°C on candy thermometer (or until a small amount of mixture "cracks" when dropped into a cup of cold water).
4 Remove from heat; allow bubbles to subside. Tilt pan slightly to one side and carefully dip an apple in toffee; twist slowly to coat apple completely. Remove apple slowly (air bubbles will form if the apples are dipped too quickly).
5 Twirl apple around a few times over pan to drain excess, then place on prepared tray. Repeat with remaining apples and toffee. Stand toffee apples at room temperature until set.
6 Place in paper cases and wrap in cellophane or use cellophane bags.

prep + cook time 40 minutes **makes** 12
tips Toffee apples can be made up to two days ahead. Store in an airtight container in a cool, dry place; do not refrigerate. Cellophane bags are available from fabric and craft stores.

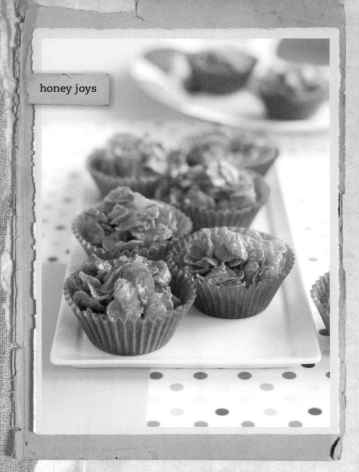

honey joys

candied popcorn

2 tablespoons vegetable oil
½ cup (110g) popping corn
2 cups (440g) caster (superfine) sugar
1 cup (250ml) water
½ teaspoon pink, green or blue food colouring

1 Heat oil in large heavy-based saucepan; cook
corn over high heat, covered with a tight-fitting
lid, shaking pan occasionally, until popping
stops. Transfer to large bowl.
2 Combine sugar, the water and colouring in
medium heavy-based frying pan; stir over heat,
without boiling, until sugar dissolves. Bring
to the boil; boil, uncovered, about 15 minutes
or until a teaspoon of mixture "cracks" when
dropped into a glass of cold water.
3 Remove pan from heat. When bubbles
subside, add popcorn; stir to coat with
toffee mixture.
4 When popcorn mixture has candied, spread
onto foil-lined oven tray to cool.

prep + cook time 30 minutes (+ cooling)
makes 6 cups
tips Use food colouring of your choice.
Popcorn can be made two days ahead; store in
an airtight container at room temperature.

honey joys

75g (2½ ounces) butter
⅓ cup (115g) honey
1 tablespoon caster (superfine) sugar
5 cups (200g) cornflakes

1 Preheat oven to 180°C/350°F. Line two 12-hole
(⅓-cup/80ml) muffin pans with paper cases.
2 Combine butter, honey and sugar in small
saucepan; stir over low heat until smooth.
3 Place cornflakes in large bowl, add butter
mixture; stir until cornflakes are well coated.
4 Divide cornflake mixture among cases; bake
8 minutes. Stand 15 minutes or until firm.

prep + cook time 20 minutes (+ standing)
makes 24
tips Honey joys can be made one day
ahead; store in an airtight container
at room temperature.

candied popcorn

cupcakes

2½ cups (375g) self-raising flour
250g (8 ounces) butter, softened
2 teaspoons vanilla extract
1¼ cups (275g) caster (superfine) sugar
5 eggs
½ cup (125ml) milk
m&ms or smarties to decorate
butter cream
200g (6½ ounces) butter, softened
2 teaspoons vanilla extract
3 cups (480g) icing (confectioners') sugar
⅓ cup (80ml) milk

1 Preheat oven to 180°C/350°F. Line two 12-hole
(⅓-cup/80ml) muffin pans with 22 paper cases.
2 Place sifted flour, butter, extract, sugar,
eggs and milk in medium bowl; beat on low
speed with electric mixer until ingredients
are just combined. Increase speed to medium;
beat about 2 minutes or until mixture has
changed to a paler colour.
3 Drop ¼ cup of mixture into each paper case.
Bake cakes about 20 minutes. Stand cakes in
pan 5 minutes before turning, top-side up, onto
wire racks to cool.
4 Meanwhile, make butter cream.
5 Spread the top of each cupcake with butter
cream. Decorate with the m&ms or smarties,
as you like.
butter cream Beat butter in medium bowl
with electric mixer until as white as possible.
Beat in extract, then sifted icing sugar and
milk, in two batches.

prep + cook time 45 minutes **makes** 22
tips Cupcakes can be made up to a day
ahead; store in an airtight container in a cool
place. Un-iced cakes are suitable to freeze.

cupcakes

toffee-on-a-stick

6 wooden ice-block sticks
1½ cups (330g) caster (superfine) sugar
½ cup (125ml) water
1 tablespoon malt vinegar
hundreds and thousands

1 Grease 12-hole (1-tablespoon/20ml) mini muffin pan. Cut ice-block sticks in half crossways.
2 Combine sugar, the water and vinegar in medium saucepan; stir over low heat until sugar dissolves. Bring to the boil; boil, uncovered, without stirring, about 15 minutes or until a small amount of mixture "cracks" when dropped into a cup of cold water.
3 Remove from heat; allow bubbles to subside. Pour toffee mixture into pan holes; sprinkle with hundreds and thousands.
4 Stand toffees about 10 minutes; place sticks, cut-side down, into centre of toffees. Stand toffees at room temperature until set.

prep + cook time 30 minutes (+ standing)
makes 12

tips For easy pouring, use a saucepan with a pouring lip or carefully transfer the hot toffee to a heatproof jug.
Toffee can be made two days ahead; store, in single layer, in an airtight container at room temperature.

fudge-frosted chocolate cupcakes

2 cups (500ml) hot water
¾ cup (75g) cocoa powder
250g (8 ounces) butter, softened
2 cups (440g) caster (superfine) sugar
2 teaspoons vanilla extract
3 eggs
1½ cups (225g) plain (all-purpose) flour
1 cup (150g) self-raising flour
½ teaspoon bicarbonate of soda (baking soda)
silver cachous
fudge frosting
50g (1½ ounces) butter, softened
¼ cup (60ml) milk
1 teaspoon vanilla extract
¼ cup (25g) cocoa powder
2 cups (320g) icing (confectioners') sugar

1 Preheat oven to 180°C/350°F. Line two 12-hole (⅓-cup/80ml) muffin pans with paper cases.
2 Whisk the water and sifted cocoa together in medium bowl.
3 Beat butter, sugar and extract in large bowl with electric mixer until light and fluffy; beat in eggs, one at a time. Fold in half the combined sifted flours and soda, then half the cocoa mixture; stir in remaining flour mixture and cocoa mixture until just combined.
4 Divide mixture among paper cases; bake about 25 minutes. Cool cakes in pans 5 minutes before transferring to wire racks to cool.
5 Meanwhile, make fudge frosting.
6 Spread frosting over cakes; decorate with cachous.
fudge frosting Beat butter in medium bowl with electric mixer until light and fluffy. Add milk, extract, sifted cocoa and half the sifted icing sugar; beat about 5 minutes or until light and fluffy. Add remaining sifted icing sugar; beat a further 5 minutes.

prep + cook time 1 hour 10 minutes **makes** 24

toffee-on-a-stick

fudge-frosted
chocolate cupcakes

chewy chocolate slice

chewy chocolate slice

125g (4 ounces) butter, melted
1 cup (220g) firmly packed light brown sugar
1 egg, beaten lightly
1 teaspoon vanilla extract
½ cup (75g) plain (all-purpose) flour
¼ cup (35g) self-raising flour
2 tablespoons cocoa powder
½ cup (45g) desiccated coconut
1 tablespoon desiccated coconut, extra
chocolate icing
1 cup (160g) icing (confectioners') sugar
2 tablespoons cocoa powder
10g (½ ounce) butter, melted
1½ tablespoons hot water, approximately

1 Preheat oven to 180°C/350°F. Grease
20cm x 30cm (8-inch x 12-inch) rectangular
pan; line base and long sides with baking paper,
extending paper 5cm (2 inches) over sides.
2 Combine butter, sugar, egg and extract in
medium bowl. Stir in sifted flours and
cocoa powder, then coconut. Spread mixture
evenly over base of pan.
3 Bake about 30 minutes.
4 Meanwhile, make chocolate icing.
5 Spread hot slice with chocolate icing;
sprinkle with extra coconut. Cool in pan
before cutting.
chocolate icing Sift icing sugar and cocoa
powder into medium bowl; add combined
butter and the water, stir until icing is a
spreadable consistency.

prep + cook time 50 minutes (+ cooling)
makes 12
tip Store in an airtight container at room
temperature for up to a week.

crunchy bubble bars

crunchy bubble bars

4 cups (180g) coco pops
250g (8 ounces) dark eating (semi-sweet)
  chocolate, chopped coarsely
100g (3 ounces) butter, chopped coarsely
¼ cup (60ml) light corn syrup

1 Grease 20cm x 30cm (8-inch x 12-inch)
rectangular pan; line base and long sides
with baking paper, extending paper
5cm (2 inches) over sides.
2 Process half the coco pops until coarse.
3 Stir chocolate, butter and syrup in large
heatproof bowl over large saucepan of
simmering water until smooth. Remove
from heat; stir in all coco pops.
4 Spread mixture into pan; refrigerate until
set. Cut into bars.

prep + cook time 20 minutes (+ refrigeration)
makes 40

coconut ice

3 Press half the mixture firmly over base of pan. Work colouring into remaining mixture; press evenly over white layer.
4 Refrigerate about 3 hours or until firm before cutting into squares.

prep + cook time 15 minutes (+ refrigeration)
makes 36
tip Coconut ice can be made a week ahead; store in an airtight container in the refrigerator.

marshmallow treats

200g (6½ ounces) butter
395g (12½ ounces) canned sweetened condensed milk
1 cup (200g) firmly packed light brown sugar
¼ cup (25g) cocoa powder
2 teaspoons vanilla extract
3¾ cups (375g) plain sweet biscuit crumbs
300g (9½ ounces) pink and white marshmallows
1½ cups (135g) desiccated coconut

1 Combine butter, condensed milk, sugar, sifted cocoa and extract in medium saucepan; stir over low heat until smooth. Remove from heat; stir in biscuit crumbs.
2 Using damp hands, roll three heaped teaspoons of mixture around each marshmallow, pressing firmly to enclose marshmallows. Place coconut in small shallow bowl; roll balls in coconut, place on trays. Refrigerate until firm.

prep + cook time 30 minutes (+ refrigeration)
makes 55

coconut ice

3½ cups (560g) icing (confectioners') sugar
2½ cups (200g) desiccated coconut
395g (12½ ounces) canned sweetened condensed milk
1 teaspoon vanilla extract
pink food colouring

1 Grease deep 19cm (8-inch) square cake pan; line base and sides with baking paper.
2 Sift icing sugar into large bowl; stir in coconut, condensed milk and extract.

marshmallow treats

gingerbread men

You obviously need a gingerbread-man cutter to make this shape but any decorative cutter – star, diamond, heart or whatever shape you already have in your kitchen – can be used for this recipe.

gingerbread men

125g (4 ounces) butter
⅓ cup (75g) firmly packed light brown sugar
½ cup (175g) golden syrup or treacle
3 cups (450g) plain (all-purpose) flour
2 teaspoons each ground ginger and
   ground cinnamon
½ teaspoon ground cloves
2 teaspoons bicarbonate of soda (baking soda)
1 egg, beaten lightly
1 teaspoon vanilla extract
royal icing
1 egg white
1 cup (160g) pure icing (confectioners') sugar
food colourings

1 Preheat oven to 180°C/350°F. Grease oven trays.
2 Heat butter, sugar and golden syrup, in small microwave-safe bowl, uncovered, on HIGH (100%) in microwave oven about 1 minute or until butter has melted. Using oven mitts, remove bowl from microwave oven; cool butter mixture 5 minutes.
3 Sift combined flour, spices and soda into large bowl; add butter mixture, egg and extract, stir with wooden spoon until combined.

4 Divide dough in half; knead each portion of dough on floured surface. Using rolling pin, roll dough out to 5mm (¼-inch) thickness. Using gingerbread-man cutter, cut out shapes; place on oven trays.
5 Bake gingerbread men about 10 minutes or until golden brown. Cool on trays.
6 Make royal icing. Decorate gingerbread men with royal icing.
royal icing Beat egg white in small bowl with electric mixer until just frothy; gradually add sifted icing sugar, beating between additions, until stiff peaks form. Tint icing, as desired, using various food colourings.

prep + cook time 50 minutes **makes** 20
tips If the mixture in step 3 is dry and crumbly, add a little more beaten egg – enough to make it feel like play dough.
To make a quick piping bag, cut off a corner of a small plastic bag.
decorating ideas You could also use coloured cachous or mini smarties to make buttons or other patterns.

chunky chewy choc-chip cookies

1 cup (220g) firmly packed light brown sugar
½ cup (110g) caster (superfine) sugar
1½ cups (225g) self-raising flour
½ cup (75g) plain (all-purpose) flour
1 cup (150g) coarsely chopped macadamias, roasted
185g (6 ounces) butter, melted, cooled
1 egg, beaten lightly
1 egg yolk, beaten lightly
2 teaspoons vanilla extract
200g (6½ ounces) dark eating (semi-sweet) chocolate,
   chopped coarsely

1 Preheat oven to 180°C/350°F.
2 Combine sugars, sifted flours and nuts in large bowl.
3 Add combined butter, egg, egg yolk and extract; mix
to a soft dough. Stir in chocolate.
4 Place level tablespoonfuls of biscuit dough, about 5cm
(2 inches) apart, on lightly greased oven trays.
5 Bake about 12 minutes or until browned lightly. Cool on trays.

prep + cook time 50 minutes **makes** 20
tips Store cookies in an airtight container for up to two weeks
at room temperature. Suitable to freeze for up to three months.

50c

chunky chewy
choc-chip cookies

chocolate fudge

1½ cups (330g) caster (superfine) sugar
½ cup (110g) firmly packed light brown sugar
60g (2 ounces) dark eating (semi-sweet)
   chocolate, chopped coarsely
2 tablespoons glucose syrup
½ cup (125ml) pouring cream
¼ cup (60ml) milk
40g (1½ ounces) unsalted butter,
   chopped coarsely

1 Grease deep 15cm (6-inch) square cake pan; line base and sides with baking paper, extending paper 5cm (2 inches) over sides.
2 Combine sugars, chocolate, glucose, cream and milk in small heavy-based saucepan; stir over low heat, without boiling, until sugar dissolves. Bring to the boil; boil, uncovered, without stirring, about 10 minutes or until mixture reaches 116°C/235°F on a candy thermometer.
3 Remove pan from heat immediately; leave candy thermometer in the mixture. Add butter; do not stir.
4 Cool fudge about 20 minutes or until the temperature of the mixture drops to 40°C/80°F; remove candy thermometer.
5 Stir fudge with wooden spoon about 10 minutes or until a small amount dropped from the spoon holds its shape.
6 Quickly spread fudge into pan; cover with foil. Stand at room temperature about 3 hours or until set.
7 Lift fudge out of pan; cut into squares approximately 2cm (¾ inch).

prep + cook time 55 minutes (+ standing)
makes 49
tip It is important to use a candy thermometer in this recipe to get the correct consistency when making the fudge.

chocolate raspberry brownies

150g (4½ ounces) butter, chopped coarsely
350g (11 ounces) dark eating (semi-sweet)
  chocolate, chopped coarsely
1 cup (220g) caster (superfine) sugar
2 eggs
1¼ cups (185g) plain (all-purpose) flour
½ cup (75g) self-raising flour
200g (6½ ounces) fresh or frozen raspberries
2 teaspoons cocoa powder

1 Preheat oven to 180°C/350°F. Grease deep
20cm (8-inch) square cake pan; line base
and sides with baking paper, extending
paper 5cm (2 inches) over edges.

2 Combine butter and 200g (6½ ounces) of
the chocolate in medium saucepan; stir over
low heat until smooth. Cool 10 minutes.
3 Stir sugar, eggs, sifted flours, raspberries
and remaining chopped chocolate into
chocolate mixture; spread into pan. Bake
about 45 minutes. Cool brownie in pan before
cutting into 16 slices.
4 Serve brownies dusted with sifted cocoa.

prep + cook time 1 hour 10 minutes **makes** 16
tip If using frozen raspberries, don't thaw
them before adding to the mixture, otherwise
they'll bleed and won't retain their shape.

chocolate raspberry brownies

choc-vanilla noughts & crosses

125g (4 ounces) butter, softened
½ cup (110g) caster (superfine) sugar
1 egg
1 teaspoon vanilla extract
1⅔ cups (250g) plain (all-purpose) flour
2 tablespoons cocoa powder
2 teaspoons milk
⅓ cup (50g) white choc bits
⅓ cup (50g) dark choc bits

1 Preheat oven to 180°C/350°F. Line oven trays with baking paper.
2 Beat butter, sugar, egg and extract in small bowl with electric mixer until combined; stir in sifted flour, in two batches.

3 Divide dough in half; stir sifted cocoa and milk into one portion. Cover; refrigerate dough 30 minutes.
4 Roll dough portions, separately, between sheets of baking paper until 5mm (¼ inch) thick. Cut 15x 6cm (2¼-inch) rounds from each; place about 2.5cm (1 inch) apart on trays.
5 Press white chocolate on chocolate rounds to make crosses; press dark chocolate on vanilla rounds to make noughts. Bake about 15 minutes; cool on trays.

prep + cook time 40 minutes (+ refrigeration)
makes 30
tips You need 96 white and 96 dark Choc Bits to make the noughts and crosses for these biscuits. Store biscuits in an airtight container at room temperature for up to a week.

patty cakes with glacé icing

125g (4 ounces) butter, softened
½ teaspoon vanilla extract
¾ cup (165g) caster (superfine) sugar
3 eggs
2 cups (300g) self-raising flour
¼ cup (60ml) milk
glacé icing
2 cups (320g) icing (confectioners') sugar
20g (¾ ounce) butter, melted
2 tablespoons hot water, approximately

1 Preheat oven to 180°C/350°F. Line 12-hole
(⅓-cup/80ml) muffin pan with paper cases.
2 Place ingredients in medium bowl; beat with
electric mixer on low speed until ingredients
are combined. Increase speed to medium; beat
about 3 minutes or until mixture is smooth
and paler in colour.
3 Divide mixture among paper cases. Bake
about 25 minutes. Stand cakes 5 minutes
before turning, top-side up, onto wire racks
to cool.
4 Meanwhile, make glacé icing.
5 Spread cakes with icing.
glacé icing Sift icing sugar into small bowl;
stir in butter and enough of the water to
make a firm paste. Stir over small saucepan
of simmering water until icing is spreadable.

prep + cook time 45 minutes **makes** 12

cake variations
berry & orange Stir in 1 teaspoon finely grated
orange rind and ½ cup dried mixed berries at
end of step 2.
citrus Stir in ½ teaspoon each of finely grated
lime, orange and lemon rind at end of step 2.
passionfruit & white chocolate Stir in ¼ cup
passionfruit pulp and ½ cup white choc bits at
end of step 2.

icing variations
coconut & lime Stir in ½ teaspoon coconut
extract and 1 teaspoon finely grated lime rind.
orange Stir in 1 teaspoon finely grated orange
rind. Replace 1 tablespoon of the hot water
with orange juice.
passionfruit Stir in 1 tablespoon passionfruit pulp.

coconut ice cakes

coconut ice cakes

60g (2 ounces) butter, softened
½ teaspoon coconut extract
½ cup (110g) caster (superfine) sugar
1 egg
¼ cup (20g) desiccated coconut
¾ cup (110g) self-raising flour
½ cup (120g) sour cream
2 tablespoons milk
coconut ice frosting
1 cup (160g) icing (confectioners') sugar
⅔ cup (50g) desiccated coconut
1 egg white, beaten lightly
pink food colouring

1 Preheat oven to 180°C/350°F. Line 18 holes
of two 12-hole (2-tablespoon/40ml) deep flat-
based patty pans with paper cases.
2 Beat butter, extract, sugar and egg in small
bowl with electric mixer until light and fluffy.
Stir in coconut, sifted flour, sour cream and
milk, in two batches. Divide mixture among
paper cases.
3 Bake cakes about 20 minutes. Stand cakes
5 minutes before turning, top-side up, onto
wire rack to cool.
4 Meanwhile, make coconut ice frosting.
5 Drop alternate rounded teaspoons of
white and pink frosting onto cakes; marble
over the top of each cake.
coconut ice frosting Sift icing sugar into
medium bowl; stir in coconut and egg white.
Place half the mixture in small bowl; tint
with pink food colouring.

prep + cook time 1 hour **makes** 18
tip Use a hot wet palette knife to spread the
frosting over cakes.

creamy caramels

1 cup (220g) caster (superfine) sugar
90g (3 ounces) unsalted butter
2 tablespoons golden syrup or treacle
⅓ cup (115g) glucose syrup
½ cup (125ml) sweetened condensed milk

1 Grease deep 19cm (8-inch) square cake pan.
2 Combine sugar, butter, golden syrup, glucose
and condensed milk in medium saucepan;
stir over heat, without boiling, until sugar
dissolves. Bring to the boil; boil, stirring, about
7 minutes or until mixture is a caramel colour.
3 Remove from heat; allow bubbles to subside.
Pour into pan; stand at room temperature
10 minutes. Mark into squares approximately
2cm (¾ inch) using greased metal spatula. Cool
completely before cutting.

prep + cook time 20 minutes (+ standing)
makes 81

creamy caramels

chocolate coconut rough slice

⅓ cup (50g) self-raising flour
⅓ cup (50g) plain (all-purpose) flour
2 tablespoons cocoa powder
⅔ cup (50g) desiccated coconut
¾ cup (165g) firmly packed light brown sugar
90g (3 ounces) unsalted butter, melted
250g (8 ounces) milk eating chocolate, melted
coconut rough filling
1½ cups (240g) icing (confectioners') sugar
1½ cups (120g) desiccated coconut
2 tablespoons cocoa powder
⅔ cup (160ml) sweetened condensed milk
75g (2½ ounces) unsalted butter, melted
1 teaspoon vanilla extract

1 Preheat oven to 180°C/350°F. Grease 20cm x 30cm (8-inch x 12-inch) rectangular pan; line base and long sides with baking paper, extending paper 5cm (2 inches) over sides.
2 Combine sifted flours and cocoa, coconut, sugar and butter in medium bowl; press mixture evenly over base of pan. Bake about 20 minutes. Cool 15 minutes.
3 Meanwhile, make coconut rough filling.
4 Spread filling evenly over warm base; top with melted chocolate. Refrigerate 2 hours or until firm.
coconut rough filling Combine ingredients in medium bowl.

prep + cook time 45 minutes (+ cooling & refrigeration) **makes** 16
tip Slice can be stored in an airtight container in the refrigerator for up to a week.

banana cupcakes with maple cream frosting

60g (2 ounces) butter, softened
60g (2 ounces) cream cheese, softened
¾ cup (165g) firmly packed light brown sugar
2 eggs
½ cup (125ml) milk
2 tablespoons maple syrup
1½ cups (225g) self-raising flour
½ teaspoon bicarbonate of soda (baking soda)
2 medium bananas (400g), halved lengthways, sliced thinly
maple cream frosting
30g (1 ounce) butter, softened
80g (2½ ounces) cream cheese, softened
2 tablespoons maple syrup
1½ cups (240g) icing (confectioners') sugar

1 Preheat oven to 180°C/350°F. Line 12-hole (⅓-cup/80ml) muffin pan with paper cases.
2 Beat butter, cream cheese and sugar in medium bowl with electric mixer until light and fluffy. Beat in eggs, one at a time. Stir in milk, syrup and sifted dry ingredients; fold in bananas.
3 Drop ¼ cup of mixture into each paper case; bake about 30 minutes. Stand cakes in pans 5 minutes before turning, top-side up, onto wire rack to cool.
4 Meanwhile, make maple cream frosting.
5 Spread cakes with frosting.
maple cream frosting Beat butter, cream cheese and syrup in small bowl with electric mixer until light and fluffy; beat in sifted icing sugar, in two batches, until combined.

prep + cook time 40 minutes **makes** 12

chocolate coconut
rough slice

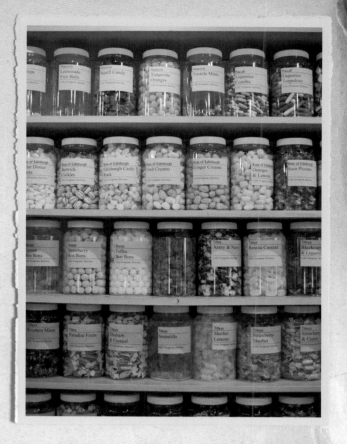

banana cupcakes with
maple cream frosting

chocolate freckle slice

Freckles are small chocolate discs covered with hundreds and thousands (nonpareils). They are available from most supermarkets and confectionery stores.

chocolate freckle slice

185g (6 ounces) butter, softened
220g (7 ounces) chocolate hazelnut spread
⅓ cup (75g) firmly packed light brown sugar
1¾ cups (250g) plain (all-purpose) flour
200g (6½ ounces) freckles

1 Preheat oven to 160°C/325°F. Grease 20cm x 30cm (8-inch x 12-inch) rectangular pan; line base and long sides with baking paper, extending paper 5cm (2 inches) over sides.
2 Beat butter, spread and sugar in small bowl with electric mixer until combined. Stir in sifted flour, in two batches.
3 Press dough into pan; smooth surface with spatula. Bake 25 minutes. Remove pan from oven; working quickly, press freckles firmly onto slice in rows about 2cm (¾ inch) apart. Cool slice in pan before cutting.

prep + cook time 45 minutes **makes** 35

peanut butter cookies

125g (4 ounces) butter, softened
¼ cup (70g) crunchy peanut butter
¾ cup (165g) firmly packed light brown sugar
1 egg
1½ cups (225g) plain (all-purpose) flour
½ teaspoon bicarbonate of soda (baking soda)
½ cup (70g) roasted unsalted peanuts, chopped coarsely

1 Preheat oven to 180°C/350°F. Grease oven trays; line with baking paper.
2 Beat butter, peanut butter, sugar and egg in small bowl with electric mixer until smooth; do not overmix. Transfer mixture to medium bowl; stir in sifted flour and soda, then nuts.
3 Roll level tablespoons of mixture into balls; place 5cm (2 inches) apart on trays, flatten with floured fork. Bake about 12 minutes; cool on trays.

prep + cook time 25 minutes **makes** 30

apricot choc-chip
muesli bars

passionfruit
marshmallows

apricot choc-chip muesli bars

125g (4 ounces) butter, chopped
½ cup (110g) firmly packed light brown sugar
1 tablespoon honey
2¼ cups (200g) rolled oats
¼ cup (40g) sunflower kernels
¼ cup (20g) desiccated coconut
½ teaspoon ground cinnamon
½ cup (75g) chopped dried apricots
2 tablespoons dark choc bits

1 Preheat oven to 160°C/325°F. Grease 20cm x 30cm (8-inch x 12-inch) rectangular pan; line base and long sides with baking paper, extending paper 5cm (2 inches) over sides.
2 Combine butter, sugar and honey in medium saucepan; stir over low heat until sugar dissolves.
3 Transfer butter mixture to medium bowl; stir in oats, sunflower kernels, coconut, cinnamon and apricots.
4 Press mixture into prepared pan; sprinkle with choc bits.
5 Bake about 30 minutes or until top is browned lightly.
6 Cut into bars while still warm; cool in pan.

prep + cook time 45 minutes (+ cooling)
makes 8
tip Store slice in an airtight container at room temperature for up to a week.

passionfruit marshmallows

2 cups (160g) desiccated coconut
⅓ cup (80ml) passionfruit pulp
1 tablespoon (14g) gelatine
¼ cup (60ml) cold water
1 cup (220g) caster (superfine) sugar
½ cup (125ml) hot water

1 Grease two 12-hole (1-tablespoon/20ml) mini muffin pans. Sprinkle inside of pan holes with a little of the coconut; shake pan to coat base and side of holes.
2 Strain passionfruit pulp into small bowl; discard seeds.
3 Sprinkle gelatine over the cold water in small bowl.
4 Stir passionfruit juice, sugar and the hot water in small heavy-based saucepan over low heat until sugar dissolves; bring to the boil. Stir in gelatine mixture; boil, without stirring, 15 minutes. Transfer to small bowl of electric mixer; cool to lukewarm.
5 Beat mixture with electric mixer, on high speed, about 4 minutes or until mixture is thick and holds its shape.
6 Working quickly, spoon the mixture into pan holes; sprinkle marshmallows with a little of the coconut to cover tops evenly. Stand at room temperature about 2 hours or until firm.
7 Place remaining coconut on large tray; gently toss marshmallows to coat in coconut.

prep + cook time 40 minutes (+ cooling & standing) makes 24
tips You need four passionfruit to get the required amount of pulp.
Store marshmallows in an airtight container at room temperature for up to two weeks.

'TIS THE SEASON

cranberry and apple fruit mince 86
stained-glass christmas cookies 89
christmas cookies...90
angel gift tag cookies 90
jaffa panforte...92
fig and nut logs...92
rocky road christmas trees 95
spiced yo-yos with brandy butter..96
fig mince pies 99
gingerbread christmas trees..100
lemon-glazed christmas wreaths...103
white christmas slice 103
chocolate panettone..105
little christmas cakes 106
little gift cakes 106
boiled christmas pudding 108
boiled fruit cake 111
little chocolate christmas puddings 111
mini christmas puddings 112
grand marnier christmas cake 115
rich chocolate christmas cakes 116
christmas star cakes 119
chocolate drambuie fruit cake..120

'TIS THE SEASON

Whether you're looking for gift ideas, edible decorations or a centrepiece for the festive table, you'll find something in this chapter. There is traditional fare, such as fruit mince and boiled fruit cake, as well as such unusual offerings as jaffa panforte and spiced yo-yos with brandy butter. Children and adults alike will delight in the rocky road Christmas trees, stained-glass Christmas cookies and angel gift tag cookies – decorations good enough to eat!

cranberry and apple fruit mince

tips Fruit mince will keep in the refrigerator for at least 12 months. If you can't find dried cherries, use the equivalent amount of extra dried cranberries instead.

cranberry and apple fruit mince

2⅔ cups (350g) dried cranberries
2½ cups (185g) finely chopped dried apples
2 cups (340g) finely chopped raisins
1 cup (150g) finely chopped dried cherries
¾ cup (150g) finely chopped dried figs
½ cup (85g) mixed peel
½ cup (115g) glacé ginger, chopped finely
3 medium apples (450g), peeled,
    grated coarsely
1½ cups (330g) firmly packed light brown sugar
½ cup (160g) raspberry jam
1 tablespoon finely grated orange rind
¼ cup (60ml) orange juice
2 teaspoons mixed spice
½ teaspoon ground cloves
1 cinnamon stick, halved
1⅓ cups (330ml) orange-flavoured liqueur

1 Mix ingredients in large bowl until combined. Cover bowl with plastic wrap.
2 Store mixture in a cool dry place for a month before using; stir mixture thoroughly every two or three days.

prep time 45 minutes (+ standing)
makes 9½ cups

cranberry and apple fruit mince

stained-glass christmas cookies

1 vanilla bean
250g (8 ounces) butter, softened
¾ cup (165g) caster (superfine) sugar
1 egg
1 tablespoon water
2¼ cups (335g) plain (all-purpose) flour
90g (3 ounces) individually wrapped sugar-free
   fruit drops, assorted colours

1 Split vanilla bean in half lengthways; scrape
seeds into medium bowl with butter, sugar, egg
and the water. Beat with electric mixer until
combined. Stir in sifted flour, in two batches.
Knead dough on floured surface until smooth.
Cover; refrigerate 30 minutes.
2 Preheat oven to 180°C/350°F. Line oven trays
with baking paper.
3 Using a rolling pin, gently tap the wrapped
lollies to crush them slightly. Unwrap lollies;
separate by colour into small bowls.

4 Roll dough between sheets of baking paper
to 5mm (¼-inch) thickness. Cut shapes from
dough using 8cm (3¼-inch) long Christmas
tree cutter; place cookies on oven trays. Using
a 4cm (1½-inch) long Christmas tree or 1.5cm
(¾-inch) star cutter, cut out the centre of each
tree to make windows. Use a skewer to make
a small hole in top of each tree for threading
through ribbon, if you like.
5 Bake trees 7 minutes. Remove trays from
oven; fill each window with a few of the same-
coloured lollies. Bake a further 5 minutes or
until browned lightly. Cool trees on trays.

prep + cook time 50 minutes (+ refrigeration)
makes 32

angel gift tag cookies

Store cookies in an airtight container for up to two days to keep them crisp until you want to attach them to your gifts.

angel gift tag cookies

125g (4 ounces) butter, softened
¾ cup (165g) caster (superfine) sugar
1 egg
1¾ cups (260g) plain (all-purpose) flour
⅓ cup (50g) self-raising flour
2 tablespoons coarse white sugar crystals
red ribbon
lemon royal icing
2 cups (320g) pure icing (confectioners') sugar
1 egg white
2 teaspoons lemon juice

1 Beat butter, caster sugar and egg in small bowl with electric mixer until light and fluffy. Stir in sifted flours, in two batches. Knead dough on floured surface until smooth. Cover; refrigerate 30 minutes.
2 Preheat oven to 180°C/350°F. Line oven trays with baking paper.
3 Roll dough between sheets of baking (parchment) paper to 5mm (¼-inch) thickness. Cut 20 x 8cm x 11cm (3¼-inch x 4½-inch) angel shapes from dough; cut two 2cm (¾-inch) moon shapes across centre of angel shapes for threading ribbon. Place angels on oven trays.
4 Bake angels about 12 minutes. Cool cookies on trays.
5 Meanwhile, make lemon royal icing.
6 Spread angels with icing; sprinkle with sugar crystals. Stand icing at room temperature until set; thread ribbon through holes.
lemon royal icing Sift icing sugar through fine sieve onto sheet of baking paper. Beat egg white in small bowl with electric mixer until foamy; beat in icing sugar, one tablespoon at a time. Stir in juice.

prep + cook time 50 minutes (+ refrigeration & standing) **makes** 20

christmas cookies

250g (8 ounces) butter, softened
¾ cup (165g) caster (superfine) sugar
1 egg
2¼ cups (335g) plain (all-purpose) flour
2 tablespoons cinnamon sugar

1 Grease oven trays; line with baking paper.
2 Beat butter, sugar and egg in small bowl with electric mixer until light and fluffy; transfer to large bowl. Stir in sifted flour.
3 Knead dough on floured surface until smooth. Cover; refrigerate 30 minutes.
4 Preheat oven to 180°C/350°F. Roll heaped teaspoons of mixture into 15cm (6-inch) log shapes. Twist two pieces of dough together; shape into canes and wreaths. Place on trays.
5 Bake cookies about 12 minutes. Sprinkle hot cookies with cinnamon sugar; cool on trays

prep + cook time 30 minutes (+ refrigeration)
makes 28

christmas cookies

jaffa panforte

⅔ cup (100g) plain (all-purpose) flour
1 cup (190g) coarsely chopped dried figs
1 cup (140g) coarsely chopped seeded
 dried dates
2 slices (45g) finely chopped glacé orange
1 cup (160g) blanched almonds, roasted
1 cup (140g) roasted hazelnuts
1 cup (140g) roasted unsalted macadamias
⅓ cup (115g) honey
⅔ cup (150g) firmly packed brown sugar
2 tablespoons orange-flavoured liqueur
100g (3 ounces) dark eating (semi-sweet)
 chocolate, melted
4 slices glacé orange (90g)

1 Preheat oven to 150°C/300°F. Grease four
deep 10cm (4-inch) round cake pans; line bases
with baking paper.
2 Sift flour into large bowl; stir in figs, dates,
chopped glacé orange and nuts.
3 Stir honey, sugar and liqueur in small
saucepan over low heat, without boiling, until
sugar dissolves. Simmer, uncovered, without
stirring, 5 minutes. Pour hot syrup, then
chocolate into nut mixture; mix well.
4 Press mixture firmly into pans; top each
with a slice of glacé orange.
5 Bake panforte about 25 minutes; cool in
pans. Remove panforte from pans; wrap in
foil. Stand overnight at room temperature.

prep + cook time 1 hour (+ standing) makes 4

fig and nut logs

150g (4½ ounces) dark eating
 (semi-sweet) chocolate
1 cup (190g) coarsely chopped dried figs
¾ cup (100g) dried cherries
1 teaspoon finely grated orange rind
¼ cup (60ml) brandy
⅔ cup (90g) coarsely chopped roasted
 unsalted pistachios
⅔ cup (70g) coarsely chopped roasted walnuts
⅓ cup (60g) finely chopped candied
 clementines
¼ cup (45g) finely chopped glacé ginger
½ teaspoon ground cinnamon
¼ teaspoon mixed spice
2 sheets (15cm x 23cm/6 inches x 9½ inches)
 edible rice paper

1 Chop half the chocolate finely. Chop
remaining chocolate coarsely, then melt in
small heatproof bowl over small saucepan
of simmering water.
2 Process figs, cherries, rind and half
the brandy until fruit is chopped finely.
Transfer mixture to large bowl; stir in nuts,
clementines, ginger, spices, and chopped and
melted chocolate.
3 Spoon mixture down long side of each rice
paper sheet. Roll each sheet to enclose filling
and make a log shape. Pinch along top of
each log to make a triangle shape; brush rice
paper with remaining brandy.
4 Wrap fruit and nut logs in baking paper;
stand overnight at room temperature. Serve
logs sliced thickly.

prep + cook time 45 minutes (+ standing)
makes 2 logs (each log serves 20)
tip Candied clementines are available from
specialty food stores and delicatessens; if you
can't find them, use glacé oranges instead.

jaffa panforte

fig and nut logs

rocky road christmas trees

rocky road christmas trees

75g (2½ ounces) unsalted butter,
   chopped coarsely
75g (2½ ounces) white eating chocolate,
   chopped coarsely
⅓ cup (75g) caster (superfine) sugar
⅓ cup (80ml) milk
⅓ cup (50g) plain (all-purpose) flour
¼ cup (35g) self-raising flour
1 egg
rocky road
100g (3 ounces) toasted marshmallows
   with coconut, cut into 1cm (½-inch) pieces
200g (6½ ounces) turkish delight,
   chopped coarsely
½ cup (70g) roasted unsalted pistachios
450g (14½ ounces) white eating
   chocolate, melted

1 Preheat oven to 160°C/325°F. Grease 8cm x 26cm (3¼-inch x 10½-inch) bar cake pan; line base and sides with baking paper, extending paper 5cm (2 inches) over sides.
2 Combine butter, chocolate, sugar and milk in small saucepan; stir over low heat until smooth. Transfer to medium bowl; cool 10 minutes. Whisk flours, then egg, into chocolate mixture. Spread mixture into pan; bake about 45 minutes, cool in pan.
3 Trim top of cake to make flat; cut four 4.5cm (1¾-inch) rounds from cake. Chop cake scraps into 1cm (½-inch) pieces; reserve.

4 Cut four 30cm (12-inch) circles from baking paper. Fold each circle in half, then roll into a cone shape, making sure the point of cone is closed tightly. Staple or tape cone securely to hold its shape.
5 Make rocky road. Spoon rocky road into cones; press down firmly to pack tightly. Press one cake round into base of each cone for a tree stump. Stand each cone upright in a tall narrow glass. Refrigerate about 1 hour or until set.
6 Remove paper from trees; serve upright on cake base.
rocky road Combine marshmallow, turkish delight, nuts and reserved chopped cake in large bowl; stir in chocolate.

prep + cook time 1 hour 25 minutes (+ cooling & refrigeration) **makes 4**

spiced yo-yos with brandy butter

250g (8 ounces) unsalted butter, softened
½ cup (110g) firmly packed dark brown sugar
1½ cups (225g) plain (all-purpose) flour
½ cup (75g) cornflour (cornstarch)
2 teaspoons ground ginger
1 teaspoon mixed spice
¼ teaspoon ground cloves
brandy butter
100g (3 ounces) unsalted butter, softened
⅔ cup (110g) icing (confectioners') sugar
2 tablespoons brandy

1 Preheat oven to 160°C/325°F. Grease oven trays; line with
baking paper.
2 Beat butter and sugar in small bowl with electric mixer until
light and fluffy; stir in sifted dry ingredients, in two batches.
3 Roll rounded teaspoons of mixture into balls. Place 3cm
(1¼ inches) apart on trays; flatten slightly using back of a
fork. Bake about 15 minutes; cool on trays.
4 Meanwhile, make brandy butter.
5 Sandwich biscuits with brandy butter.
brandy butter Beat butter and sifted icing sugar in small
bowl with electric mixer until light and fluffy. Beat in
brandy until combined.

prep + cook time 40 minutes (+ cooling) **makes** 32

Regular light brown sugar can be used
instead of dark brown sugar. Unfilled
yo-yos will keep well for about a week in
an airtight container. Once filled, the yo-yos
will keep in the refrigerator for a few days.

spiced yo-yos with
brandy butter

fig mince pies

fig mince pies

150g (4½ ounces) dried figs, chopped finely
½ cup (65g) dried cranberries
½ cup (75g) raisins, chopped coarsely
¼ cup (40g) mixed peel
¼ cup (55g) finely chopped glacé ginger
¼ cup (60g) finely chopped glacé peach
1 medium apple (150g), grated coarsely
½ cup (110g) firmly packed light brown sugar
2 tablespoons fig jam
1 teaspoon finely grated orange rind
2 tablespoons orange juice
1 cinnamon stick, halved
1 teaspoon mixed spice
⅓ cup (80ml) brandy
1½ sheets shortcrust pastry
1 egg white
pastry
2 cups (300g) plain (all-purpose) flour
⅓ cup (75g) caster (superfine) sugar
150g (4½ ounces) cold butter, chopped coarsely
1 egg, beaten lightly

fig mince pies

1 Combine fruit, sugar, jam, rind, juice, spices and brandy in medium bowl. Cover; stand for one week or up to one month. Stir mixture every two or three days.
2 Make pastry.
3 Grease two 12-hole (2-tablespoon/40ml) deep flat-based patty pans. Divide pastry in half; roll one portion of dough between sheets of baking paper to 3mm (⅛-inch) thickness; cut 12 x 7cm (2¾-inch) rounds from pastry. Repeat with remaining pastry. Press rounds into pan holes; prick bases all over with fork, refrigerate 30 minutes.
4 Preheat oven to 200°C/400°F.
5 Cut whole pastry sheet into 16 squares; cut each square into six strips. Cut the half pastry sheet into eight squares; cut each square into six strips.
6 Use six strips to make a lattice pattern. Cut a 6.5cm (2½-inch) round from latticed pastry. Repeat with remaining pastry strips.

7 Discard cinnamon stick from mince. Spoon mince into pastry cases; top with lattice pastry rounds. Press edges to seal; brush pastry with egg white. Bake about 20 minutes. Dust with a little sifted icing sugar if you like before serving.
pastry Blend or process flour, sugar and butter until crumbly. Add egg; process until combined. Knead pastry on floured surface until smooth. Cover; refrigerate 30 minutes.

prep + cook time 1 hour 40 minutes
(+ standing & refrigeration) **makes** 24
tips Mince pies will keep well in an airtight container for up to two weeks. Make double the quantity of fruit mince to bottle for gifts.

gingerbread christmas trees

3 cups (450g) self-raising flour
¾ cup (165g) firmly packed light brown sugar
1 tablespoon ground ginger
1 teaspoon each ground cinnamon and
    ground nutmeg
½ teaspoon ground cloves
185g (6 ounces) butter, chopped coarsely
¾ cup (270g) golden syrup or treacle
1 egg
silver cachous
1 tablespoon icing (confectioners') sugar
royal icing
1 egg white
1½ cups (240g) pure icing
    (confectioners') sugar

1 Process flour, brown sugar, spices and butter until crumbly. Add golden syrup and egg; process until combined. Knead dough on floured surface until smooth. Cover; refrigerate 1 hour.
2 Divide dough in half; roll each half between sheets of baking paper to 5mm (¼-inch) thickness. Refrigerate 30 minutes.
3 Preheat oven to 180°C/350°F. Line oven trays with baking paper.
4 Cut 12 x 3cm (1¼-inch), 12 x 5cm (2-inch), 12 x 6cm (2¼-inch), 12 x 7cm (2¾-inch), 12 x 8cm (3¼-inch) and 12 x 9cm (3¾-inch) stars from dough; transfer stars to trays. You will need to reroll the dough several times to get the correct number of stars.
5 Bake 3cm, 5cm and 6cm stars about 10 minutes and remaining stars about 12 minutes.
6 Meanwhile, make royal icing.
7 Assemble trees by joining two 9cm stars, two 8cm stars, two 7cm stars, two 6cm stars, two 5cm stars and two 3cm stars with a little royal icing between each star. Decorate trees by joining cachous to stars with a tiny dot of royal icing. Dust trees with sifted icing sugar.
royal icing Sift icing sugar through fine sieve. Beat egg white until foamy in small bowl with electric mixer; beat in icing sugar, 1 tablespoon at a time.

prep + cook time 1 hour 20 minutes
(+ refrigeration & cooling) **makes** 6
tips The trees will keep for several weeks in airtight containers. You will have a lot of royal icing left over; use it for making snow on the trees, if you like, or halve the recipe.

gingerbread christmas trees

white christmas slice

white christmas slice

500g (1 pound) white eating chocolate,
  chopped coarsely
1 cup (35g) rice bubbles
1 cup (160g) sultanas
1 cup (80g) desiccated coconut
⅔ cup (110g) finely chopped dried apricots
½ cup (100g) halved red glacé cherries

1 Grease 20cm x 30cm (8-inch x 12-inch)
rectangular pan; line base and long sides with
baking paper, extending paper 5cm (2 inches)
over sides.
2 Melt chocolate in large heatproof bowl set
over large saucepan of simmering water.
Remove from heat; quickly stir in remaining
ingredients.
3 Press mixture firmly into pan. Refrigerate
2 hours or until firm before cutting.

prep time 20 minutes (+ refrigeration)
makes 32

lemon-glazed christmas wreaths

3 cups (450g) self-raising flour
125g (4 ounces) butter
¼ cup (60ml) milk
⅔ cup (110g) caster (superfine) sugar
1 teaspoon vanilla extract
2 eggs
silver edible glitter
lemon icing
3 cups (480g) icing (confectioners') sugar
2 tablespoons lemon juice, approximately

1 Preheat oven to 180°C/350°F. Grease oven trays; line
with baking paper.
2 Sift flour into medium bowl; rub in butter. Combine
milk and sugar in small saucepan; stir over low heat
until sugar dissolves. Add extract; cool 5 minutes. Stir
combined warm milk mixture and eggs into flour mixture.
3 Knead dough on floured surface until smooth.
4 Roll rounded teaspoons of dough into 13cm (5¼-inch)
sausages. Twist two sausages together, form into circles;
press edges together. Place about 2.5cm (1 inch) apart
on oven trays.
5 Bake about 15 minutes. Transfer to wire racks to cool.
6 Meanwhile, make lemon icing.
7 Drizzle wreaths with icing; set at room temperature.
Sprinkle with edible glitter.
lemon icing Sift icing sugar into small heatproof bowl;
stir in enough juice to make a thick paste. Stir over
small saucepan of simmering water until pourable.

prep + cook time 35 minutes (+ cooling) makes 30

lemon-glazed
christmas wreaths

chocolate panettone

chocolate panettone

¾ cup (180ml) warm milk
1 teaspoon caster (superfine) sugar
1 tablespoon dried yeast
2¼ cups (335g) plain (all-purpose) flour
⅓ cup (35g) cocoa powder
¼ cup (55g) caster (superfine) sugar, extra
1 teaspoon coarse cooking salt (kosher salt)
1 teaspoon vanilla extract
50g (1½ ounces) butter, softened
2 eggs
2 egg yolks
½ cup (90g) raisins
⅓ cup (45g) coarsely chopped seeded
  dried dates
½ cup (95g) dark choc bits
1 egg, extra
2 teaspoons icing (confectioners') sugar

1 Combine milk, caster sugar and yeast in medium jug. Cover; stand in warm place about 10 minutes or until frothy.

2 Sift flour, cocoa, extra caster sugar and salt into large bowl; stir in yeast mixture, extract, butter, eggs, yolks, fruit and choc bits. Knead dough on floured surface about 10 minutes or until elastic. Place dough in greased large bowl. Cover; stand in warm place about 1 hour or until doubled in size.

3 Preheat oven to 200°C/400°F. Line 6-hole (¾-cup/180ml) texas muffin pan with paper cases. To make your own, cut six 15cm (6-inch) squares from baking paper. Cut six 15cm (6-inch) squares from photocopier paper. Line pan first with paper, then with baking paper, set at a different angle.

4 Knead dough on floured surface about 10 minutes or until dough loses its stickiness. Divide dough into six equal portions and press into pan holes. Cover loosely; stand in warm place about 30 minutes or until doubled in size. Brush panettone with extra egg.

5 Bake panettone about 25 minutes. Stand in pan 5 minutes; turn, top-side up, onto wire rack to cool. Dust with sifted icing sugar.

prep + cook time 1 hour (+ standing) **makes** 6.

little christmas cakes

2 cups (320g) sultanas
1 cup (160g) dried currants
1 cup (150g) raisins, chopped coarsely
1 cup (140g) seeded dates, chopped coarsely
1 cup (200g) dried figs, chopped coarsely
¼ cup (50g) red glacé cherries,
   chopped coarsely
½ cup (160g) glacé fruit (such as pineapple,
   apricot, peach), chopped coarsely
¾ cup (180ml) brandy
250g (8 ounces) butter, softened
1 cup (220g) firmly packed dark brown sugar
¼ cup (85g) orange marmalade
4 eggs
1¾ cups (260g) plain (all-purpose) flour
½ cup (75g) self-raising flour
1½ teaspoons ground cinnamon
1 teaspoon mixed spice
green glacé cherries, to decorate
sugared almonds, to decorate
lemon icing
3 cups (480g) pure icing (confectioners') sugar
¼ cup (60ml) water
1 tablespoon lemon juice

1 Combine fruit in large bowl; stir in ½ cup of
the brandy. Cover; stand in a cool, dark place
overnight or up to one week, stirring every day.
2 Preheat oven to 160°C/325°F. Lightly grease
20 holes of two 12-hole (⅓-cup/80ml) muffin
pans. Line bases with baking paper.
3 Beat butter, sugar and marmalade in
small bowl with electric mixer until combined.
Beat in eggs, one at a time. Transfer mixture
to large bowl; stir in sifted dry ingredients, in
two batches. Stir in fruit mixture.
4 Divide mixture among pan holes; smooth
tops. Bake about 30 minutes. Brush hot cake
tops with remaining brandy.
5 Stand cakes in pans 5 minutes before
turning, top-side up, onto wire rack to cool.
6 Meanwhile, make lemon icing.
7 Working quickly, spoon a heaped tablespoon
of warm icing over each cake. Press cherry
or almond in centre of each cake; stand cakes
until icing sets.
lemon icing Sift icing sugar into microwave-
safe bowl. Add enough of the water and
juice to make a thick paste. Microwave,
uncovered, on HIGH (100%) 20-30 seconds or
until warm and of a pouring consistency.

prep + cook time 1 hour 15 minutes (+ standing
& cooling) **makes** 20
tip If icing thickens, microwave again about
10 seconds or until it's of a pouring consistency.

little gift cakes

1 x 19cm (7½-inch) square fruit cake
1kg (2 pounds) ready-made white icing
icing (confectioners') sugar, for dusting
food colourings
¾ cup (240g) apricot jam, warmed, sieved
ribbons, to decorate

1 Cut cake into nine equal pieces; cover to
keep airtight.
2 Knead icing on surface dusted with sifted
icing sugar, until smooth. Divide icing into nine
equal portions. Tint icing by kneading food
colourings into portions, as desired. Wrap
each piece of icing individually in plastic wrap
until ready to use.
3 Brush top and sides of cake evenly with jam
just before it is ready to be covered with icing.
Roll icing between sheets of baking paper until
large enough to cover top and sides of cake.
Lift icing onto cake, then lightly mould icing
over cake with hands dusted in icing sugar;
trim edges neatly.
4 Repeat with remaining icing and cakes. Icing
scraps can be cut to make decorative shapes;
secure shapes to cakes with a little more jam.
Decorate cakes with ribbons.

prep time 1 hour 30 minutes **makes** 9
tip Use plain white icing, if you prefer.

little christmas cakes

little gift cakes

boiled christmas pudding

1½ cups (250g) raisins
1½ cups (240g) sultanas
1 cup (150g) dried currants
¾ cup (120g) mixed peel
1 teaspoon finely grated lemon rind
2 tablespoons lemon juice
2 tablespoons brandy
250g (8 ounces) butter, softened
2 cups (440g) firmly packed light brown sugar
5 eggs
1¼ cups (185g) plain (all-purpose) flour
½ teaspoon each ground nutmeg and
   mixed spice
4 cups (280g) stale breadcrumbs

1 Combine fruit, rind, juice and brandy in large bowl. Cover; store in a cool dark place overnight or up to one week, stirring every day.
2 Beat butter and sugar in large bowl with electric mixer until combined. Beat in eggs, one at a time. Stir butter mixture into fruit mixture. Stir in sifted dry ingredients and breadcrumbs.
3 Fill large boiler three-quarters full of hot water. Cover; bring to the boil. Have ready 2.5m (8 feet) of kitchen string and an extra ½ cup of plain flour. Wearing thick rubber gloves, dip pudding cloth in boiling water; boil 1 minute, then remove and carefully squeeze excess water from cloth. Working quickly, spread hot cloth on bench; rub flour into centre of cloth to cover an area about 40cm (16 inches) in diameter, leaving flour a little thicker in centre of cloth where "skin" on the pudding needs to be thickest.

4 Place pudding mixture in centre of cloth. Gather cloth evenly around mixture, avoiding any deep pleats; pat into round shape. Tie cloth tightly with string, as close to mixture as possible. Pull ends of cloth tightly to ensure pudding is as round and firm as possible. Knot two pairs of corners together to make pudding easier to remove.
5 Lower pudding into boiling water; tie free ends of string to handles of boiler to suspend pudding. Cover with tight-fitting lid; boil for 6 hours, replenishing water as necessary to maintain level.
6 Untie pudding from handles; place wooden spoon through knotted cloth loops to lift pudding from water. Do not put pudding on bench; suspend from spoon by placing over rungs of upturned stool or wedging handle in drawer. Pudding must be suspended freely. Twist ends of cloth around string to avoid them touching pudding. If pudding has been cooked correctly, cloth will dry in patches within a few minutes; hang 10 minutes.
7 Place pudding on board; cut string, carefully peel back cloth. Turn pudding onto a plate, then carefully peel cloth away completely; cool. Stand at least 20 minutes or until skin darkens and pudding becomes firm.

prep + cook time 6 hours 30 mins (+ standing & cooling) **serves** 16

boiled christmas pudding

boiled fruit cake

little chocolate
christmas puddings

boiled fruit cake

5 cups (1kg) mixed dried fruit,
  chopped coarsely
250g (8 ounces) butter, chopped coarsely
1¼ cups (275g) firmly packed light
  brown sugar
1 cup (250ml) sherry
¼ cup (60ml) water
2 teaspoons finely grated orange rind
4 eggs, beaten lightly
1½ cups (225g) plain (all-purpose) flour
½ cup (75g) self-raising flour
2 teaspoons mixed spice
½ cup (60g) pecans
¾ cup (105g) unsalted macadamias

1 Grease deep 22cm (9-inch) round cake pan;
line base and side with three thicknesses of
baking paper, extending paper 5cm (2 inches)
above side.
2 Combine fruit, butter, sugar, ¾ cup of the
sherry and the water in large saucepan; stir
over medium heat until butter is melted and
sugar dissolved. Bring to the boil; remove from
heat. Transfer to large bowl; cool.
3 Preheat oven to 150°C/300°F.
4 Stir rind and eggs into fruit mixture, then
sifted dry ingredients. Spread mixture into pan;
top with nuts.
5 Bake cake about 3 hours. Brush hot cake
with remaining sherry. Cover with foil; cool in
pan overnight.

prep + cook time 3½ hours (+ cooling)
serves 20
tip This is a rich cake and will keep well. Store
it in the fridge in an airtight container.

little chocolate christmas puddings

700g (1½ pounds) plum pudding
250g (8 ounces) dark eating (semi-sweet)
  chocolate, melted
½ cup (125ml) brandy
½ cup (80g) icing (confectioners') sugar
200g (6½ ounces) white chocolate melts
red and green glacé cherries, cut to resemble
  berries and leaves

1 Crumble pudding into large bowl. Stir
in melted chocolate, brandy and sifted icing
sugar; mix well.
2 Roll level tablespoons of mixture into balls;
place on tray. Cover; refrigerate until firm.
3 Melt white chocolate in small heatproof bowl
over small saucepan of simmering water. Cool
chocolate 10 minutes. Drizzle over puddings to
form "custard"; decorate with cherries.

prep + cook time 45 minutes (+refrigeration)
makes 45
tips You can use either bought or leftover
homemade pudding. This recipe can be made
two weeks ahead.

mini christmas puddings

1 cup (150g) raisins, chopped coarsely
1 cup (160g) sultanas
1 cup (150g) finely chopped seeded dried dates
½ cup (95g) finely chopped seeded prunes
½ cup (85g) mixed peel
½ cup (125g) finely chopped glacé apricots
1 teaspoon finely grated lemon rind
2 tablespoons lemon juice
2 tablespoons apricot jam
2 tablespoons brandy
250g (8 ounces) butter, softened
2 cups (440g) firmly packed light brown sugar
5 eggs
1¼ cups (185g) plain (all-purpose) flour
½ teaspoon each ground nutmeg and
   mixed spice
4 cups (280g) stale breadcrumbs
1 cup (150g) plain flour, extra
6 x 30cm (12-inch) squares unbleached calico

1 Combine fruit, rind, juice, jam and brandy in large bowl. Cover; stand in cool, dark place for one week, stirring every day.
2 Beat butter and sugar in small bowl with electric mixer until combined; beat in eggs, one at a time. Stir butter mixture into fruit mixture. Stir in sifted dry ingredients and breadcrumbs.
3 Fill boiler three-quarters full of hot water, cover with tight lid; bring to the boil. Have ready 1m (3 feet) of kitchen string, plus extra flour. Wearing thick rubber gloves, dip pudding cloths, one at a time, into boiling water; boil 1 minute, then remove. Squeeze excess water from cloth. Spread hot cloths on bench; rub 2 tablespoons of the extra flour into centre of each cloth to cover an area about 18cm (7 inches) in diameter, leaving flour a little thicker in centre of cloth where "skin" on the pudding needs to be thickest.

4 Divide pudding mixture equally among cloths; placing in centre of each cloth. Gather cloths around mixture, avoiding any deep pleats; pat into round shapes. Tie cloths tightly with string, as close to mixture as possible. Tie loops in string. Lower three puddings into the boiling water. Cover; boil 2 hours, replenishing with boiling water as necessary to maintain water level.
5 Lift one pudding from water, using wooden spoons through string loops. Do not put pudding on bench; suspend from spoon by placing over rungs of upturned stool or wedging the spoon in a drawer. Twist ends of cloth around string to avoid them touching pudding; hang 10 minutes. Repeat with remaining puddings.
6 Place puddings on board; cut string, carefully peel back cloth. Turn puddings onto plates, then carefully peel cloth away completely; cool. Stand at least 20 minutes or until skin darkens and pudding becomes firm.

prep + cook time 4 hours 50 minutes (+ standing) makes 6
tips This recipe makes six generous single servings. You need six 30cm squares of unbleached calico for each pudding cloth. If the calico has not been used before, soak it in cold water overnight; the next day, boil it for 20 minutes, then rinse in cold water. Puddings can be cooked in two boilers or in batches; the mixture will keep at room temperature for several hours.
Top puddings with a slice of glacé orange, if you like. It is available from gourmet and health-food stores.

mini christmas puddings

grand marnier christmas cake

grand marnier christmas cake

3 cups (500g) sultanas
½ cup (100g) glacé cherries
1½ cups (250g) raisins, chopped coarsely
1½ cups (115g) seeded dried dates,
  chopped coarsely
½ cup (125g) glacé apricots, chopped coarsely
½ cup (125g) glacé pineapple, chopped coarsely
¼ cup (85g) orange marmalade
¾ cup (180ml) grand marnier
250g (8 ounces) butter, softened
¾ cup (165g) firmly packed dark brown sugar
4 eggs
2 cups (300g) plain (all-purpose) flour
2 teaspoons mixed spice
1 cup (160g) roasted almonds, chopped coarsely
¼ cup (60ml) grand marnier, extra
decorations
¼ cup (55g) caster (superfine) sugar
¼ cup (60ml) water
500g (1 pound) ready-made white icing
icing (confectioners') sugar, for dusting
christmas tree cutter
coloured cachous
ribbon

1 Combine fruit, marmalade and liqueur in large bowl; mix well. Cover; store mixture in cool, dark place overnight or up to one week, stirring every day.

2 Preheat oven to 150°C/300°F. Grease deep 19cm (8-inch) square cake pan; line base and sides with two layers each of brown and baking papers, extending paper 5cm (2 inches) above sides.

3 Beat butter and sugar in small bowl with electric mixer until combined. Beat in eggs, one at a time. Stir butter mixture into fruit mixture. Stir in sifted flour and spice, then nuts.

4 Spread mixture into pan. Bake about 3 hours. Brush top of hot cake with extra liqueur. Cover cake tightly with foil; turn cake upside down. Cool in pan overnight.

5 To decorate cake, combine sugar and the water in small saucepan; stir over heat until sugar dissolves. Boil, uncovered, 1 minute; cool syrup.

6 Place cake, top-side down, on board. Brush with some of the syrup.

7 Knead icing on surface dusted with sifted icing sugar, until smooth. Roll icing until large enough to cover top of cake. Lift icing onto cake; smooth with hands, trim excess icing. Stand 3 hours or overnight until firm.

8 Place cutter gently on cake to use as a guide. Brush the icing inside cutter with a little of the reserved syrup; sprinkle with cachous. Remove cutter. Decorate sides of cake with ribbon.

prep + cook time 3 hours 45 minutes
(+ standing) **serves** 16

rich chocolate christmas cakes

1 cup (170g) seeded prunes
1 cup (140g) seeded dried dates
1 cup (150g) raisins
½ cup (75g) muscatels
1 cup (200g) dried figs
5 (100g) glacé orange slices
1½ cups (375ml) irish whiskey
1½ cups (330g) firmly packed dark
   brown sugar
185g (6 ounces) butter, softened
3 eggs
½ cup (50g) ground hazelnuts
1½ cups (225g) plain (all-purpose) flour
2 tablespoons cocoa powder
1 teaspoon mixed spice
½ teaspoon ground nutmeg
½ teaspoon bicarbonate of soda (baking soda)
150g (5 ounces) dark eating (semi-sweet)
   chocolate, chopped finely
¼ cup (60ml) water
1 cup (150g) muscatels, extra
2 tablespoons cocoa powder, extra

1 Chop all fruit finely. Combine fruit and ¾ cup of the whiskey in large bowl. Cover; stand overnight.
2 Preheat oven to 120°C/250°F. Line eight deep 8cm (3¼-inch) round cake pans with two thicknesses of baking paper, extending paper 5cm (2 inches) above sides of pans.
3 Stir remaining whiskey and ¾ cup of the sugar in small saucepan over low heat until sugar dissolves; bring to the boil. Remove from heat; cool syrup 20 minutes.
4 Meanwhile, beat butter and remaining sugar in small bowl with electric mixer until combined; beat in eggs, one at a time. Stir butter mixture into fruit mixture. Stir in ground hazelnuts, sifted dry ingredients, chocolate and ½ cup of the cooled syrup. Spread mixture into pans.
5 Bake cakes about 1¾ hours.
6 Bring remaining syrup and the water to the boil in small saucepan; boil for 3 minutes or until thickened slightly. Brush hot cakes with half of the hot syrup. Cover cakes with foil; cool in pans.
7 Divide extra muscatels into eight small bunches; place bunches in remaining syrup. Stand in syrup until cool; drain.
8 Dust cakes with extra sifted cocoa; top with muscatel bunches.

prep + cook time 2½ hours (+ standing & cooling) **makes** 8
tip Buy 200g (6½ ounces) muscatels for these cakes; use one-third in the cake mixture and the rest for decorating.

rich chocolate christmas cakes

christmas star cakes

christmas star cakes

4½ cups (1.1kg) cranberry and apple fruit
mince (see page 86)
185g (6 ounces) butter, chopped coarsely
¾ cup (165g) firmly packed light brown sugar
⅓ cup (80ml) bourbon whiskey
⅓ cup (80ml) water
2 teaspoons finely grated orange rind
1 teaspoon finely grated lemon rind
1 tablespoon treacle
3 eggs
1¼ cups (185g) plain (all-purpose) flour
¼ cup (35g) self-raising flour
½ teaspoon bicarbonate of soda (baking soda)
500g (1 pound) ready-made white icing
100g (3 ounces) ready-made almond icing
1 cup (160g) icing (confectioners') sugar
1 egg white

1 Combine fruit mince, butter, brown sugar,
whiskey and the water in large saucepan. Stir
over low heat until butter melts and sugar
dissolves; bring to the boil. Remove from heat;
transfer to large heatproof bowl. Cool.
2 Preheat oven to 150°C/300°F. Line 22 holes
of two 12-hole (⅓-cup/80ml) muffin pans with
paper cases.
3 Stir rinds, treacle and eggs into fruit mixture.
Stir in sifted flours and soda. Spoon mixture
into paper cases.
4 Bake cakes about 40 minutes. Cover; cool in
pan overnight.
5 Trim top of each cake to make it flat. Knead
white icing and almond icing together on
bench dusted with some of the sifted icing
sugar, until smooth. Roll three-quarters
of the icing to 5mm (¼-inch) thickness. Cut
22 x 6.5cm (2½-inch) rounds from icing.
6 Brush top of each cake with egg white; top
with icing rounds. Roll remaining icing on
bench dusted with more sifted icing sugar to
3mm (⅛-inch) thickness. Cut out 22 stars using
a 4cm (1½-inch) cutter and 44 stars using a
2cm (1-inch) cutter. Decorate cakes with
stars by brushing each with a little egg white
to secure in position.

prep + cook time 1½ hours (+ standing
& cooling) **makes** 22

chocolate drambuie fruit cake

2⅓ cups (375g) sultanas
2¼ cups (335g) raisins, chopped coarsely
1⅔ cups (270g) dried currants
1½ cups (250g) seeded prunes, chopped coarsely
1½ cups (210g) seeded dried dates,
   chopped coarsely
¾ cup (125g) mixed peel
⅔ cup (140g) red glacé cherries, quartered
1⅓ cups (330ml) drambuie
⅓ cup (120g) honey
1 tablespoon finely grated lemon rind
250g (8 ounces) butter, softened
1½ cups (330g) firmly packed dark brown sugar
6 eggs
90g (3 ounces) dark eating (semi-sweet)
   chocolate, grated
1¼ cups (150g) pecans, chopped coarsely
2 cups (300g) plain (all-purpose) flour
1 cup (150g) self-raising flour
¼ cup (25g) cocoa powder

1 Combine fruit, 1 cup of the liqueur, honey and rind in large bowl. Cover; store in a cool, dark place overnight or up to one week, stirring every day.
2 Preheat oven to 120°C/250°F. Grease 6-hole (¾-cup/180ml) texas muffin pan. Grease deep 22cm (9-inch) round or deep 19cm (8-inch) square cake pan; line base and side(s) with four thicknesses of baking paper, extending paper 5cm (2 inches) above side(s).
3 Beat butter and sugar in medium bowl with electric mixer until combined. Beat in eggs, one at a time. Stir butter mixture into fruit mixture with chocolate and nuts. Stir in sifted dry ingredients, in two batches.
4 Fill each muffin pan hole, level to the top, with mixture; spread remaining mixture into cake pan. Decorate tops with extra pecans and glacé cherries, if you like.
5 Bake muffins about 1½ hours (cake can stand while muffins are baking). Brush hot muffins with some of the remaining liqueur; cover with foil, cool in pan.
6 Increase oven temperature to 150°C/300°F. Bake large cake about 3 hours; brush hot cake with remaining liqueur. Cover hot cake with foil; cool in pan overnight.

prep + cook time 4 hours 50 minutes
(+ standing & cooling) **serves** 36

Cake can be made up to three months ahead; store in an airtight container in the refrigerator or freeze for up to 12 months.

If you don't want to make the mini cakes, spread cake mixture into a deep 25cm (10-inch) round or deep 22cm (9-inch) square cake pan; bake about 4 to 4½ hours.

chocolate drambuie fruit cake

GRANDMA'S KITCHEN

lamingtons...126

neenish and pineapple tarts.............................129

banana bread 130

dutch ginger and almond slice.........................130

apricot squares...133

cheese and poppy seed biscuits 133

old-fashioned apple pie slice............................134

cherry bakewell tarts 137

monte carlos..137

madeleines 138

tangy lemon squares 138

jam drops..140

anzac biscuits..141

boiled chocolate cake 142

apple cinnamon tea loaves...............................145

date and walnut rolls 145

madeira cake 146

cut-and-keep buttercake..................................146

traditional shortbread......................................149

blueberry macaroon slice 150

butterfly cakes...150

fruit mince slice...152

rhubarb custard tea cake.................................154

carrot cake with cream cheese frosting.............156

mini pecan, macadamia and walnut pies 157

rock cakes...158

banana cake with passionfruit icing..................158

GRANDMA'S KITCHEN

The fragrant aroma of baking, wooden spoons to lick, the first slice of a loaf fresh from the oven – for many of us, time spent in our grandmother's kitchen was a cherished part of childhood. Take a trip down memory lane with these mouth-watering recipes for tarts, slices, cakes, loaves, biscuits and pies – just like grandma used to make.

lamingtons

6 eggs
⅔ cup (150g) caster (superfine) sugar
⅓ cup (50g) cornflour (cornstarch)
½ cup (75g) plain (all-purpose) flour
⅓ cup (50g) self-raising flour
2 cups (160g) desiccated coconut
chocolate icing
4 cups (640g) icing (confectioners') sugar
½ cup (50g) cocoa powder
15g (½ ounce) butter, melted
1 cup (250ml) milk

1 Preheat oven to 180°C/350°F. Grease 20cm x 30cm (8-inch x 12-inch) rectangular pan; line base and long sides with baking paper, extending paper 5cm (2 inches) over sides.
2 Beat eggs in large bowl with electric mixer about 10 minutes or until thick and creamy; gradually add sugar, beating until dissolved between additions. Triple-sift flours; fold into egg mixture.
3 Spread mixture into pan; bake about 35 minutes. Turn cake immediately onto baking-paper-covered wire rack to cool.
4 Meanwhile, make chocolate icing.
5 Cut cake into 16 pieces. Dip each piece in icing; drain off excess. Place coconut into medium bowl; toss squares in coconut. Place lamingtons on wire rack to set.
chocolate icing Sift icing sugar and cocoa in medium heatproof bowl; stir in butter and milk. Set bowl over medium saucepan of simmering water; stir until icing is of a coating consistency.

prep + cook time 50 minutes **makes** 16

lamingtons

neenish and pineapple tarts

neenish and pineapple tarts

1¾ cups (260g) plain (all-purpose) flour
¼ cup (40g) icing (confectioners') sugar
185g (6 ounces) cold butter, chopped coarsely
1 egg yolk
2 teaspoons iced water, approximately
2 tablespoons strawberry jam
2 tablespoons finely chopped glacé pineapple
mock cream
¾ cup (165g) caster (superfine) sugar
⅓ cup (80ml) water
1½ tablespoons milk
½ teaspoon gelatine
185g (6 ounces) unsalted butter, softened
1 teaspoon vanilla extract
glacé icing
1½ cups (240g) icing (confectioners') sugar
15g (½ ounce) unsalted butter, melted
2 tablespoons hot milk, approximately
yellow and pink food colouring
½ teaspoon cocoa powder

1 Process flour, sugar and butter until crumbly. With motor operating, add egg yolk and enough of the water to make ingredients come together. Turn dough onto floured surface; knead gently until smooth. Wrap pastry in plastic; refrigerate 30 minutes.
2 Grease two 12-hole (2-tablespoon/40ml) deep flat-based patty pans. Roll out half the pastry between sheets of baking paper until 3mm (⅛ inch) thick. Cut out 12 x 7.5cm (3-inch) rounds; press rounds into holes of one pan. Prick bases with a fork. Repeat with remaining pastry. Refrigerate 30 minutes.

3 Preheat oven to 220°C/425°F.
4 Bake cases about 12 minutes. Stand cases 5 minutes before transferring to wire rack to cool.
5 Meanwhile, make mock cream and glacé icing.
6 Divide jam among half the cases and pineapple among remaining cases. Fill cases with mock cream; level tops with spatula. Spread yellow icing over pineapple tarts. Spread pink icing over half of each jam tart; cover remaining half with chocolate icing.
mock cream Stir sugar, ¼ cup of the water and milk in small saucepan over low heat, without boiling, until sugar dissolves. Sprinkle gelatine over remaining water in small jug; stir into milk mixture until gelatine dissolves. Cool to room temperature. Beat butter and extract in small bowl with electric mixer until as white as possible. While motor is operating, gradually beat in cold milk mixture; beat until light and fluffy.
glacé icing Sift icing sugar into medium bowl; stir in butter and enough of the milk to make a thick paste. Place ⅓ cup of the icing in small heatproof bowl; tint with yellow colouring. Divide remaining icing between two small heatproof bowls; tint icing in one bowl with pink colouring and the other with sifted cocoa. Stir each bowl over small saucepan of simmering water until icing is spreadable.

prep + cook time 1 hour 10 minutes (+ refrigeration & cooling) **makes** 24

banana bread

banana bread

prep + cook time 1 hour 20 minutes serves 12
tips You need two large overripe bananas
(460g) to get the amount of mashed banana
required for this recipe.
For an authentic café experience, lightly toast
the banana bread and serve it with butter.

1 cup mashed banana
1 cup (220g) firmly packed dark brown sugar
2 eggs, beaten lightly
40g (1½ ounces) butter, melted
½ cup (125ml) buttermilk
¼ cup (90g) treacle
1½ cups (225g) plain (all-purpose) flour
1 cup (150g) self-raising flour
2 teaspoons mixed spice
1 teaspoon bicarbonate of soda (baking soda)

1 Preheat oven to 180°C/350°F. Grease 14cm x
21cm (5½-inch x 8½-inch) loaf pan; line base
and long sides with baking paper, extending
paper 5cm (2 inches) over sides.
2 Combine banana, sugar, eggs, butter,
buttermilk and treacle in large bowl; stir
in sifted dry ingredients. Do not overmix;
the batter should be lumpy. Spoon mixture
into pan.
3 Bake about 1 hour. Stand in pan 10 minutes;
turn, top-side up, onto wire rack to cool.

dutch ginger and almond slice

1¾ cups (260g) plain (all-purpose) flour
1 cup (220g) caster (superfine) sugar
⅔ cup (150g) coarsely chopped glacé ginger
½ cup (80g) blanched almonds,
  chopped coarsely
1 egg
185g (6 ounces) butter, melted
2 teaspoons icing (confectioners') sugar

1 Preheat oven to 180°C/350°F. Grease
20cm x 30cm (8-inch x 12-inch) rectangular
pan; line base and long sides with baking paper,
extending paper 5cm (2 inches) over sides.
2 Combine sifted flour, sugar, ginger, nuts
and egg in medium bowl; stir in butter.
3 Press mixture into pan; bake about
35 minutes. Stand slice in pan 10 minutes
before lifting onto wire rack to cool. Dust
with sifted icing sugar before cutting.

prep + cook time 50 minutes makes 20

dutch ginger and
almond slice

apricot squares

apricot squares

1½ cups (250g) dried apricots
500g (1 pound) plain sweet biscuits
250g (8 ounces) butter, chopped coarsely
¾ cup (165g) firmly packed light brown sugar
395g (12½ ounces) canned sweetened
  condensed milk
⅓ cup (25g) desiccated coconut

cheese and poppy
seed biscuits

1 Grease 23cm x 32cm (9-inch x 13-inch) swiss roll pan; line base and long sides with baking paper, extending paper 5cm (2 inches) over sides.
2 Process apricots until finely chopped; transfer to large bowl. Process biscuits, in two batches, until finely crushed; transfer to bowl with apricots.
3 Combine butter, sugar and condensed milk in medium saucepan; whisk over low heat until butter is melted. Bring to the boil, whisking constantly. Remove from heat; stir into apricot mixture.
4 Spread mixture into pan; smooth surface. Sprinkle with coconut; cool. Refrigerate until firm before cutting into squares or bars.

prep + cook time 30 minutes **makes** 30
tips Depending on size of the food processor, the apricots can be processed in two batches. Place saucepan over a small gas jet or element to prevent burning mixture on edge of pan.

cheese and poppy seed biscuits

100g (3 ounces) butter, softened
1 cup (120g) coarsely grated mature
  cheddar cheese
1 cup (150g) plain (all-purpose) flour
¼ teaspoon salt
¼ cup (40g) poppy seeds

1 Process butter and cheese until just combined. Add flour and salt; process until mixture comes together. Roll dough into 25cm (10-inch) log; roll log in poppy seeds. Place on tray; refrigerate 2 hours or until firm.
2 Preheat oven to 160°C/325°F. Line oven trays with baking paper.
3 Cut log into 5mm (¼-inch) thick slices; place 2.5cm (1 inch) apart on trays. Bake 15 minutes or until browned lightly. Cool on trays.

prep + cook time 35 minutes (+ refrigeration)
makes 35

old-fashioned apple pie slice

8 medium apples (1.5kg)
⅔ cup (150g) caster (superfine) sugar
½ cup (125ml) water
2 tablespoons white (granulated) sugar, optional
pastry
3 cups (450g) self-raising flour
¼ cup (40g) icing (confectioners') sugar
125g (4 ounces) cold butter, chopped coarsely
1 egg, beaten lightly
½ cup (125ml) milk, approximately
passionfruit icing
1½ cups (240g) icing (confectioners') sugar
¼ cup (60ml) passionfruit pulp, approximately

1 Peel, quarter and core apples; slice thickly. Place apples, caster sugar and the water in large saucepan; cover, bring to the boil. Reduce heat; simmer about 10 minutes or until the apples are just tender. Gently turn the apple mixture into a large colander or strainer to drain; cool to room temperature.
2 Preheat oven to 200°C/400°F. Grease 20cm x 30cm (8-inch x 12-inch) rectangular pan; line base and long sides with baking paper, extending paper 5cm (2 inches) over sides.
3 Make pastry.

4 Roll two-thirds of the pastry on floured surface until large enough to line base and sides of pan, with 1cm (½ inch) extending over sides. Lift pastry into pan. Spread cold apple mixture into pastry case; brush edges with a little extra milk. Roll out remaining pastry until large enough to generously cover pie. Place over filling; press edges together to seal. Trim excess pastry around edges. Brush top with a little milk; sprinkle with white sugar. Slash about six holes in pastry.
5 Bake pie 45 minutes. Stand in pan 10 minutes; turn, top-side up, onto wire rack to cool.
6 Meanwhile, make passionfruit icing.
7 Spread icing over pastry; serve slice cut into squares.
pastry Sift flour and icing sugar into large bowl; rub in butter. Make a well in centre. Using a knife, "cut" combined egg and enough milk through flour mixture to make a soft dough.
passionfruit icing Sift icing sugar into medium heatproof bowl, stir in enough of the passionfruit pulp to make a thick paste. Place bowl over saucepan of simmering water; stir icing until spreadable.

prep + cook time 1 hour 40 minutes (+ cooling)
serves 8
tip You will need approximately two passionfruit to make this recipe.

old-fashioned
apple pie slice

cherry bakewell tarts

monte carlos

cherry bakewell tarts

90g (3 ounces) unsalted butter, softened
2 tablespoons caster (superfine) sugar
1 egg yolk
1 cup (150g) plain (all-purpose) flour
½ cup (60g) ground almonds
2 tablespoons strawberry jam
12 red glacé cherries, halved
almond filling
125g (4 ounces) unsalted butter, softened
½ teaspoon finely grated lemon rind
½ cup (110g) caster (superfine) sugar
2 eggs
¾ cup (90g) ground almonds
2 tablespoons plain (all-purpose) flour
lemon glaze
1 cup (160g) icing (confectioners') sugar
2 tablespoons lemon juice, approximately

1 Beat butter, sugar and egg yolk in small
bowl with electric mixer until combined. Stir
in sifted flour and ground almonds, in two
batches. Turn dough onto floured surface;
knead gently until smooth. Wrap in plastic;
refrigerate 30 minutes.
2 Preheat oven to 220°C/425°F.
3 Make almond filling.
4 Grease two 12-hole (1½-tablespoon/30ml)
shallow round-based patty pans. Roll pastry
between sheets of baking paper until 3mm
(⅛ inch) thick. Cut 24 x 6cm (2¼-inch) rounds
from pastry; gently press rounds into holes in
pans. Divide jam, then filling, into cases; bake
about 20 minutes. Stand tarts 10 minutes; turn,
top-side up, onto wire rack.
5 Meanwhile, make lemon glaze.
6 Spoon glaze over warm tarts; top with
cherries. Cool.
almond filling Beat butter, rind and sugar
in small bowl with electric mixer until light
and fluffy. Beat in eggs, one at a time. Stir
in ground almonds and flour.
lemon glaze Sift icing sugar into small bowl;
stir in enough juice to make glaze pourable.

prep + cook time 1 hour (+ refrigeration
& cooling) **makes** 24

monte carlos

185g (6 ounces) unsalted butter, softened
1 teaspoon vanilla extract
½ cup (110g) firmly packed light brown sugar
1 egg
1¼ cups (185g) self-raising flour
¾ cup (110g) plain (all-purpose) flour
½ cup (40g) desiccated coconut
½ cup (160g) raspberry jam
cream filling
60g (2 ounces) unsalted butter, softened
¾ cup (120g) icing (confectioners') sugar
½ teaspoon vanilla extract
2 teaspoons milk

1 Preheat oven to 180°C/350°F. Grease
oven trays.
2 Beat butter, extract and sugar in small bowl
with electric mixer until light and fluffy.
Add egg; beat until combined. Stir in sifted
flours and coconut.
3 Shape level teaspoons of dough into oval
shapes; place about 4cm (1½ inches) apart on
trays. Roughen surface with fork.
4 Bake biscuits about 12 minutes. Cool on trays.
5 Meanwhile, make cream filling.
6 Place ½ teaspoon each of jam and cream
filling in centre of half the biscuits. Top with
remaining biscuits; gently press together.
cream filling Beat butter and icing sugar in
small bowl with electric mixer until light and
fluffy. Beat in extract and milk.

prep + cook time 50 minutes **makes** 50

madeleines

4 Drop rounded tablespoons of mixture into pan holes.
5 Bake madeleines about 10 minutes. Tap hot pan firmly on bench to release madeleines, then turn immediately onto baking-paper-covered wire racks to cool. Serve dusted with extra sifted icing sugar.

prep + cook time 25 minutes **makes** 24

tangy lemon squares

125g (4 ounces) butter, softened
¼ cup (40g) icing (confectioners') sugar
1¼ cups (185g) plain (all-purpose) flour
3 eggs
1 cup (220g) caster (superfine) sugar
2 teaspoons finely grated lemon rind
½ cup (125ml) lemon juice
2 teaspoons icing (confectioners') sugar, extra

1 Preheat oven to 180°C/350°F. Grease shallow 22cm (9-inch) square cake pan; line base and sides with baking paper, extending paper 2.5 cm (1 inch) over sides.
2 Beat butter and sifted icing sugar in small bowl with electric mixer until smooth. Stir in 1 cup of the flour.
3 Press mixture evenly over base of pan. Bake about 15 minutes or until browned lightly.
4 Meanwhile, place eggs, caster sugar, remaining flour, rind and juice in bowl; whisk until combined. Pour egg mixture over hot base.
5 Bake about 20 minutes or until firm. Cool slice in pan on a wire rack before cutting. Serve dusted with extra sifted icing sugar.

prep + cook time 55 minutes (+ cooling) **makes** 16
tips Look for lemons that are bright and heavy; they have more juice and flavour.
Store slice, covered, in the refrigerator for up to three days.

madeleines

2 eggs
2 tablespoons caster (superfine) sugar
2 tablespoons icing (confectioners') sugar
1 teaspoon vanilla extract
¼ cup (35g) self-raising flour
¼ cup (35g) plain (all-purpose) flour
75g (2½ ounces) butter, melted
1 tablespoon hot water
2 tablespoons icing (confectioners')
  sugar, extra

1 Preheat oven to 200°C/400°F. Grease two 12-hole (1½-tablespoon/30ml) madeleine pans with a little butter.
2 Beat eggs, caster sugar, sifted icing sugar and extract in small bowl with electric mixer until thick and creamy.
3 Meanwhile, sift flours twice. Sift flours over egg mixture; pour combined butter and the water down side of bowl, then fold ingredients together.

tangy lemon squares

jam drops

125g (4 ounces) butter, softened
½ teaspoon vanilla extract
½ cup (110g) caster (superfine) sugar
1 cup (120g) ground almonds
1 egg
1 cup (150g) plain (all-purpose) flour
1 teaspoon finely grated lemon rind
⅓ cup (110g) raspberry jam
2 tablespoons apricot jam

1 Preheat oven to 180°C/350°F. Line oven trays with baking paper.
2 Beat butter, extract, sugar and ground almonds in small bowl with electric mixer until light and fluffy. Beat in egg; stir in sifted flour.
3 Divide rind between both jams; mix well.
4 Roll tablespoons of mixture into balls; place about 5cm (2 inches) apart on trays, flatten slightly. Using end of a wooden spoon, press a flower shape, about 1cm (½ inch) deep, into dough. Fill each hole with a little jam, using raspberry jam for petals of flowers and apricot jam for centres.
5 Bake drops about 15 minutes. Cool on trays.

prep + cook time 40 minutes makes 24
tip Jam drops will keep in an airtight container at room temperature for up to two days.

jam drops

anzac biscuits

anzac biscuits

125g (4 ounces) butter, chopped
2 tablespoons golden syrup or treacle
1 tablespoon water
½ teaspoon bicarbonate of soda (baking soda)
1 cup (220g) firmly packed light brown sugar
½ cup (40g) desiccated coconut
1 cup (90g) rolled oats
1 cup (150g) plain (all-purpose) flour

1 Preheat oven to 160°C/325°F. Line oven trays with baking paper.
2 Stir butter, syrup and the water in large saucepan over low heat until smooth. Remove from heat; stir in soda, then remaining ingredients.
3 Roll tablespoons of mixture into balls; place about 5cm (2 inches) apart on trays, flatten slightly. Bake about 20 minutes; cool on trays.

prep + cook time 35 minutes **makes** 25

Anzacs should still feel soft when they're cooked; they will firm up as they cool. Store the biscuits in an airtight container at room temperature for up to a week.

1 Preheat oven to 180°C/350°F. Grease deep
26.5cm x 33cm (10½-inch x 13¼-inch), 3.5-litre
(14-cup) baking dish; line base with baking paper.
2 Combine the water, sugar, butter and sifted
cocoa and soda in medium saucepan; stir over
heat, without boiling, until sugar dissolves.
Bring to the boil. Reduce heat; simmer,
uncovered, 5 minutes. Transfer mixture to
large bowl; cool to room temperature.
3 Add flour and eggs to bowl; beat with electric
mixer until mixture is smooth and paler in
colour. Pour mixture into pan; bake about
50 minutes. Stand cake in pan 10 minutes before
turning, top-side up, onto wire rack to cool.
4 Meanwhile, make fudge frosting.
5 Spread cold cake with frosting.
fudge frosting Combine butter, the water
and caster sugar in small saucepan; stir
over low heat, without boiling, until sugar
dissolves. Sift icing sugar and cocoa into
small bowl, then gradually stir in hot butter
mixture. Cover; refrigerate about 20 minutes
or until frosting thickens. Beat with a
wooden spoon until spreadable.

prep + cook time 1 hour 10 minutes (+ cooling
& refrigeration) **serves** 20

boiled chocolate cake

2 cups (500ml) water
3 cups (660g) caster (superfine) sugar
250g (8 ounces) butter, chopped
⅓ cup (35g) cocoa powder
1 teaspoon bicarbonate of soda (baking soda)
3 cups (450g) self-raising flour
4 eggs
fudge frosting
90g (3 ounces) butter, chopped
⅓ cup (80ml) water
½ cup (110g) caster (superfine) sugar
1½ cups (240g) icing (confectioners') sugar
⅓ cup (35g) cocoa powder

$2

boiled chocolate cake

apple cinnamon tea loaves

date and walnut rolls

apple cinnamon tea loaves

90g (3 ounces) butter, softened
1 teaspoon vanilla extract
½ cup (110g) caster (superfine) sugar
1 egg
1⅓ cups (200g) self-raising flour
½ cup (125ml) milk
1 medium red apple (150g), quartered, cored,
   sliced thinly
15g (½ ounce) butter, melted
1 tablespoon white (granulated) sugar
½ teaspoon ground cinnamon
spiced honey cream
⅔ cup (160ml) double cream
2 teaspoons honey
¼ teaspoon ground ginger
pinch ground cinnamon

1 Preheat oven to 180°C/350°F. Grease 8-hole
(¾-cup/180ml) petite loaf pan.
2 Beat softened butter, extract and caster sugar
in small bowl with electric mixer until light
and fluffy. Add egg; beat until combined. Stir
in sifted flour and milk, in two batches.
3 Divide mixture among pan holes; top with
apple, brush with melted butter, sprinkle with
half the combined white sugar and cinnamon.
4 Bake loaves about 20 minutes. Sprinkle hot
loaves with remaining sugar and cinnamon
mixture. Stand loaves 5 minutes before turning,
top-side up, onto wire rack to cool.
5 Meanwhile, make spiced honey cream.
6 Serve warm cakes with spiced honey cream.
spiced honey cream Combine ingredients in
small bowl.

prep + cook time 35 minutes **makes** 8

date and walnut rolls

60g (2 ounces) butter
1 cup (250ml) boiling water
1 cup (180g) finely chopped dried dates
½ teaspoon bicarbonate of soda (baking soda)
1 cup (220g) firmly packed light brown sugar
2 cups (300g) self-raising flour
½ cup (60g) coarsely chopped walnuts
1 egg, beaten lightly

1 Preheat oven to 180°C/350°F. Grease two
8cm x 19cm (3¼-inch x 8-inch) nut roll tins;
line bases with baking paper. Place tins upright
on oven tray.
2 Stir butter and the water in medium
saucepan over low heat until butter melts.
Remove from heat; stir in dates and soda,
then remaining ingredients. Spoon mixture
into tins; replace lids.
3 Bake rolls about 50 minutes. Stand rolls in
tins 5 minutes. Remove ends (top and bottom);
shake tins gently to release rolls onto wire
rack to cool. Serve rolls sliced with butter.

prep + cook time 1 hour 10 mins **serves** 20
tips If you can't buy new nut roll tins, look
around secondhand shops or garage sales –
you might be lucky. They will rust if not looked
after properly, as they're made from tin.
You can also make your own nut roll tins
from tall 850ml (8cm x 17cm) fruit juice cans.
Remove one end from each can by using a
can opener that cuts just below the rims. Wash
and dry cans thoroughly before greasing.
It is important not to fill nut roll tins with too
much mixture. The nut rolls rise surprisingly
high – both because the tin is narrow and
because the cooking method approximates
that of steaming. As a rough guide, the tins
should be filled just a little over halfway.
Some nut roll tins open along the side; be
certain these are closed properly before baking.
Some lids have tiny holes in them to allow
steam to escape; make sure these are not used
on the bottoms of the tins.

madeira cake

cut-and-keep buttercake

125g (4 ounces) butter, softened
1 teaspoon vanilla extract
1¼ cups (275g) caster (superfine) sugar
3 eggs
1 cup (150g) plain (all-purpose) flour
½ cup (75g) self-raising flour
¼ teaspoon bicarbonate of soda (baking soda)
½ cup (125ml) milk

1 Preheat oven to 180°C/350°F. Grease deep
20cm (8-inch) round cake pan; line base with
baking paper.
2 Beat ingredients in medium bowl on low
speed with electric mixer until just combined.
Increase speed to medium; beat about
3 minutes or until mixture is smooth and
pale in colour.
3 Spread mixture into pan; bake about
1¼ hours. Stand cake in pan 5 minutes before
turning, top-side up, onto wire rack to cool.
Dust cake with sifted icing sugar, if desired.

prep + cook time 1 hour 30 minutes **serves** 10

madeira cake

180g (5½ ounces) butter, softened
2 teaspoons finely grated lemon rind
⅔ cup (150g) caster (superfine) sugar
3 eggs
¾ cup (110g) plain (all-purpose) flour
¾ cup (110g) self-raising flour
⅓ cup (55g) mixed peel
¼ cup (35g) slivered almonds

1 Preheat oven to 160°C/325°F. Grease deep
20cm (8-inch) round cake pan; line base
with baking paper.
2 Beat butter, rind and sugar in small bowl
with electric mixer until light and fluffy; beat
in eggs, one at a time. Transfer mixture to large
bowl; stir in sifted flours.
3 Spread mixture into pan; bake 20 minutes.
Remove cake from oven; sprinkle with peel and
nuts. Return to oven; bake about 40 minutes.
Stand cake in pan 5 minutes before turning,
top-side up, onto wire rack to cool.

prep + cook time 1 hour 15 minutes **serves** 12

cut-and-keep
buttercake

traditional shortbread

traditional shortbread

250g (8 ounces) butter, softened
⅓ cup (75g) caster (superfine) sugar 2½oz.
1 tablespoon water
2 cups (300g) plain (all-purpose) flour 10
½ cup (90g) rice flour 3oz.
2 tablespoons white (granulated) sugar

1 Preheat oven to 160°C/325°F. Grease oven trays.
2 Beat butter and caster sugar in medium bowl with electric mixer until light and fluffy; stir in the water and sifted flours, in two batches. Knead mixture on floured surface until smooth.

3 Divide mixture in half; shape each half on a separate tray into a 20cm (8-inch) round. Mark each round into 12 wedges; prick with fork. Pinch edges of rounds with fingers; sprinkle shortbread with white sugar.
4 Bake about 40 minutes; stand 5 minutes. Using sharp knife, cut into wedges along marked lines. Cool on trays.

prep + cook time 1 hour **makes** 24
tips Ground white rice can be used instead of rice flour; it is slightly coarser in texture. Store shortbread in an airtight container at room temperature for up to a week.

blueberry macaroon slice

butterfly cakes

125g (4 ounces) butter, softened
1 teaspoon vanilla extract
⅔ cup (150g) caster (superfine) sugar
3 eggs
1½ cups (225g) self-raising flour
¼ cup (60ml) milk
½ cup (160g) jam
1 cup (250ml) thickened (heavy)
   cream, whipped

1 Preheat oven to 180°C/350°F. Line two 12-hole
(2-tablespoon/40ml) deep flat-based patty pans
with paper cases.
2 Beat butter, extract, sugar, eggs, sifted flour
and milk in small bowl with electric mixer,
on low speed, until ingredients are just
combined. Increase speed to medium; beat
about 3 minutes or until mixture is smooth
and pale in colour.
3 Drop rounded tablespoons of mixture into
paper cases. Bake about 20 minutes. Stand
cakes in pans 5 minutes before turning, top-
side up, onto wire racks to cool.
4 Using small sharp knife, cut a circle from the
top of each cake; cut circle in half to make two
"wings". Fill cavities with jam and whipped
cream. Place wings in position on tops of cakes.
Dust with a little sifted icing sugar before
serving, if you like.

prep + cook time 50 minutes **makes** 24

blueberry macaroon slice

90g (3 ounces) butter, softened
½ cup (110g) caster (superfine) sugar
1 egg
⅔ cup (100g) plain (all-purpose) flour
¼ cup (35g) self-raising flour
1 tablespoon custard powder
½ cup (160g) blueberry jam
coconut topping
2 egg whites, beaten lightly
2½ cups (190g) shredded coconut
¼ cup (55g) caster (superfine) sugar

1 Preheat oven to 180°C/350°F. Grease 20cm x
30cm (8-inch x 12-inch) rectangular pan. Line
base and long sides with baking paper; extend
paper 5cm (2 inches) over sides.
2 Beat butter, sugar and egg in small bowl with
electric mixer until combined; stir in sifted
flours and custard powder. Spread dough into
pan; spread with jam.
3 Make coconut topping; sprinkle over jam.
4 Bake slice about 40 minutes; cool in pan.
coconut topping Place ingredients in medium
bowl; stir to combine.

prep + cook time 1 hour **makes** 32
tip Store slice in an airtight container at room
temperature for up to a week.

butterfly cakes

$3

fruit mince slice

1½ cups (225g) plain (all-purpose) flour
1¼ cups (185g) self-raising flour
155g (5 ounces) cold butter, chopped
1 tablespoon golden syrup or treacle
1 egg
⅓ cup (80ml) milk, approximately
2 teaspoons milk, extra
1 tablespoon demerara sugar
fruit mince
500g (1 pound) mixed dried fruit, chopped coarsely
½ cup (125ml) water
½ cup (110g) firmly packed dark brown sugar
1 tablespoon orange marmalade
2 teaspoons finely grated orange rind
2 tablespoons orange juice

1 Make fruit mince.
2 Grease 20cm x 30cm (8-inch x 12-inch) rectangular pan; line base and long sides with baking paper, extending paper 5cm (2 inches) over sides.
3 Sift flours into large bowl; rub in butter until mix is crumbly. Stir in combined syrup and egg, and enough milk to make a firm dough. Knead gently on floured surface until smooth. Refrigerate 30 minutes.
4 Preheat oven to 200°C/400°F.
5 Divide dough in half. Roll one half between sheets of baking paper until large enough to cover base of pan; press into pan, spread fruit mince over dough.
6 Roll remaining dough between sheets of baking paper until large enough to cover fruit mince; place on top of fruit mince, trim to fit. Brush with extra milk; sprinkle with demerara sugar. Bake about 20 minutes. Cool in pan before cutting.
fruit mince Combine ingredients in medium saucepan; cook, stirring, over medium heat, about 10 minutes or until thick. Cool.

prep + cook time 50 minutes (+ refrigeration & cooling) **makes** 24
tips Use white (granulated) sugar instead of the demerara, if you like.
Store slice in an airtight container at room temperature for up to a week.

fruit mince slice

rhubarb custard tea cake

200g (6½ ounces) butter, softened
½ cup (110g) caster (superfine) sugar
2 eggs
1¼ cups (185g) self-raising flour
⅓ cup (40g) custard powder
4 fresh rhubarb stalks (300g), sliced lengthways,
    then cut into 10cm (4-inch) lengths
20g (¾ ounce) butter, melted
2 teaspoons caster (superfine) sugar, extra
custard
2 tablespoons custard powder
¼ cup (55g) caster (superfine) sugar
1 cup (250ml) milk
20g (¾ ounce) butter
2 teaspoons vanilla extract

1 Make custard.
2 Preheat oven to 180°C/350°F. Grease deep 20cm (8-inch) round cake pan; line base with baking paper.
3 Beat softened butter and sugar in small bowl with electric mixer until light and fluffy. Beat in eggs, one at a time. Transfer to medium bowl; stir in sifted flour and custard powder.
4 Spread half the mixture into pan; spread custard over cake mixture. Dollop small spoonfuls of remaining cake mixture over custard; carefully spread with spatula to completely cover custard. Top cake mixture with rhubarb; brush gently with melted butter, then sprinkle with extra sugar.
5 Bake cake about 1¼ hours; cool in pan.
custard Combine custard powder and sugar in small saucepan; gradually stir in milk. Cook, stirring, until mixture boils and thickens slightly. Remove from heat; stir in butter and extract. Press plastic wrap over surface of custard to prevent a skin forming; cool. Whisk until smooth before using.

prep + cook time 1 hour 50 minutes (+ cooling)
serves 8

rhubarb custard
tea cake

carrot cake with lemon cream cheese frosting

1 cup (250ml) vegetable oil
1⅓ cups (295g) firmly packed light
    brown sugar
3 eggs
3 cups firmly packed, coarsely grated carrot
1 cup (110g) coarsely chopped walnuts
2½ cups (375g) self-raising flour
½ teaspoon bicarbonate of soda (baking soda)
2 teaspoons mixed spice
lemon cream cheese frosting
30g (1 ounce) butter, softened
80g (2½ ounces) cream cheese, softened
1 teaspoon finely grated lemon rind
1½ cups (240g) icing (confectioners') sugar

1 Preheat oven to 180°C/350°F. Grease deep 22cm (9-inch) round cake pan; line base with baking paper.
2 Beat oil, sugar and eggs in small bowl with electric mixer until thick and creamy. Transfer mixture to large bowl; stir in carrot, nuts, then sifted dry ingredients.
3 Pour mixture into pan; bake about 1¼ hours. Stand cake in pan 5 minutes before turning, top-side up, onto wire rack to cool.
4 Meanwhile, make lemon cream cheese frosting. Spread cake with frosting.
lemon cream cheese frosting Beat butter, cream cheese and rind in small bowl with electric mixer until light and fluffy. Gradually beat in sifted icing sugar.

prep + cook time 1 hour 45 minutes **serves** 12
tip You will need three large carrots (540g) to make this recipe.

carrot cake with
lemon cream
cheese frosting

mini pecan, macadamia and walnut pies

1¼ cups (185g) plain (all-purpose) flour
⅓ cup (55g) icing (confectioners') sugar
¼ cup (30g) ground almonds
125g (4 ounces) cold butter, chopped coarsely
1 egg yolk
filling
⅓ cup (50g) unsalted macadamias, roasted
⅓ cup (45g) pecans, roasted
⅓ cup (35g) walnuts, roasted
2 tablespoons light brown sugar
1 tablespoon plain (all-purpose) flour
40g (1½ ounces) butter, melted
2 eggs, beaten lightly
¾ cup (180ml) maple syrup

mini pecan, macadamia and walnut pies

1 Grease four 10cm (4-inch) round loose-based flan tins.
2 Blend or process flour, icing sugar, ground almonds and butter until crumbly. Add egg yolk; process until ingredients just come together. Knead dough on floured surface until smooth. Cover; refrigerate 30 minutes.
3 Divide pastry into quarters. Roll each piece, between sheets of baking paper, into rounds large enough to line prepared tins; lift pastry into tins. Press into sides; trim edges. Cover; refrigerate 30 minutes.
4 Meanwhile, preheat oven to 200°C/400°F.
5 Place tins on oven tray. Line each tin with baking paper; fill with dried beans or rice. Bake 10 minutes. Remove paper and beans. Bake about 7 minutes or until browned lightly.
6 Meanwhile, make filling.
7 Reduce oven temperature to 180°C/350°F.
8 Divide filling among cases. Bake about 25 minutes or until set; cool.
filling Combine ingredients in medium bowl; mix well.

prep + cook time 1 hour (+ refrigeration)
makes 4
tips Do not use maple-flavoured syrup as a substitute for the "real thing" in the nut filling. To roast nuts, place in a heavy-based frying pan and stir constantly over medium-to-high heat, until they are evenly browned. Remove from pan immediately.

rock cakes

rock cakes

2 cups (300g) self-raising flour
¼ teaspoon ground cinnamon
⅓ cup (75g) caster (superfine) sugar
90g (3 ounces) cold butter, chopped
1 cup (160g) sultanas
1 egg, beaten lightly
½ cup (125ml) milk
1 tablespoon caster sugar, extra

1 Preheat oven to 200°C/400°F. Grease oven trays.
2 Sift flour, cinnamon and sugar into medium bowl; rub in butter. Stir in sultanas, egg and milk; do not overmix.
3 Drop rounded tablespoons of mixture, about 5cm (2 inches) apart, onto trays; sprinkle with extra sugar. Bake about 15 minutes; cool cakes on trays.

prep + cook time 30 minutes **makes** 18

banana cake with passionfruit icing

160g (5 ounces) butter, softened
¾ cup (165g) firmly packed light brown sugar
2 eggs
1½ cups (350g) mashed banana
1 teaspoon bicarbonate of soda (baking soda)
2 tablespoons hot milk
1 cup (150g) plain (all-purpose) flour
⅔ cup (100g) self-raising flour
passionfruit icing
1 cup (160g) icing (confectioners') sugar
2 tablespoons passionfruit pulp, approximately

1 Preheat oven to 180°C/350°F. Grease deep 20cm (8-inch) round cake pan; line base and side with baking paper.
2 Beat butter and sugar in small bowl with electric mixer until light and fluffy. Beat in eggs, one at a time. Transfer mixture to large bowl; stir in banana. Combine soda and milk in small jug; stir into banana mixture. Stir in sifted flours, in two batches. Spread mixture into pan.
3 Bake about 45 minutes. Stand cake in pan 5 minutes before turning, top-side up, onto wire rack to cool.
4 Meanwhile, make passionfruit icing. Drizzle cake with icing.
passionfruit icing Sift icing sugar into small bowl; stir in enough of the passionfruit pulp until icing is pourable.

prep + cook time 1 hour 15 minutes **serves** 10
tip You need three large overripe bananas (690g) to get the amount of mashed banana required for this recipe.

banana cake with passionfruit icing

$3

JAMS AND PRESERVES

fruit butters 164
spicy mustard pickles 167
fig and quince paste 167
peach chutney 168
green mango chutney 168
traditional italian tomato pasta sauce................................171
apple jelly 173
dark plum jam..173
spicy chilli paste (harissa) 174
marinated mushrooms 175
quince jelly 176
marinated capsicums...176
spiced fig and apple jam...181
rhubarb chutney...181
pink grapefruit marmalade 182
sweet chilli sauce 184
whisky seville marmalade...184
sweet orange marmalade 187
strawberry conserve..187
chilli jam..189
tomato chutney 190
preserved lemons 190
dukkah...193

JAMS AND PRESERVES

No pantry is complete without a shelf of homemade spreads and condiments. Jars are filled with sweet jams, savoury pickles and sauces, marinated vegies, fruity chutneys and exotic offerings, such as chilli-hot harissa and spicy dukkah. All lined up in a row, they're as pretty as a picture as well.

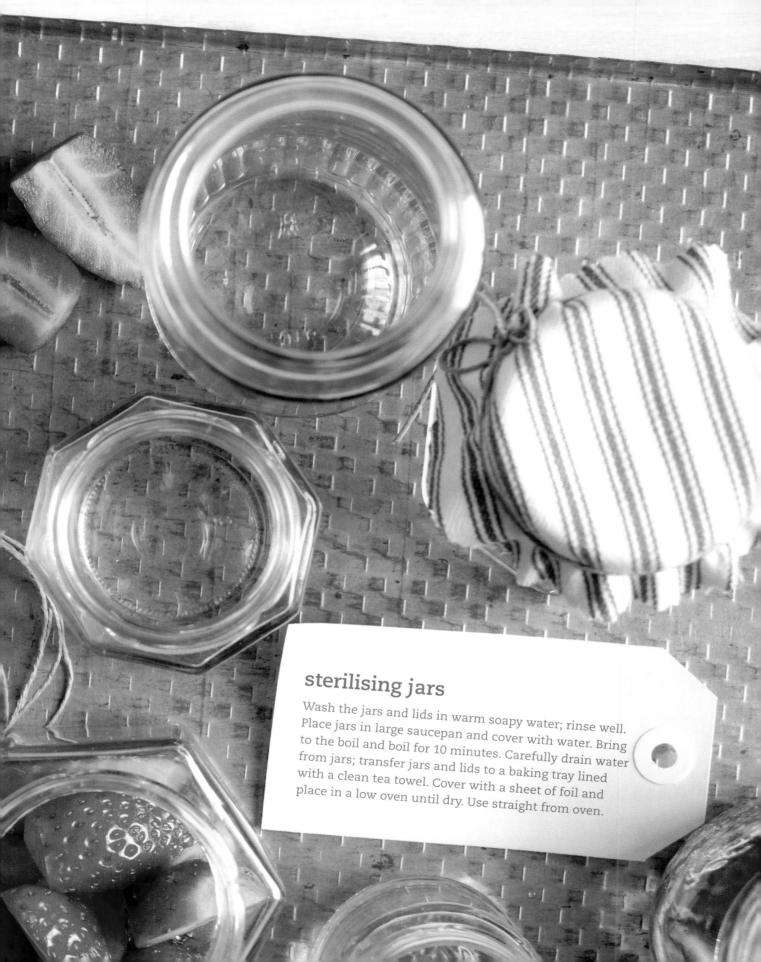

sterilising jars

Wash the jars and lids in warm soapy water; rinse well. Place jars in large saucepan and cover with water. Bring to the boil and boil for 10 minutes. Carefully drain water from jars; transfer jars and lids to a baking tray lined with a clean tea towel. Cover with a sheet of foil and place in a low oven until dry. Use straight from oven.

fruit butters

passionfruit butter
4 eggs, beaten lightly, strained
185g (6 ounces) unsalted butter, chopped
¾ cup (165g) caster (superfine) sugar
⅓ cup (80ml) lemon juice
1 cup (250ml) passionfruit pulp
lime butter
4 eggs, beaten lightly, strained
185g (6 ounces) unsalted butter, chopped
1½ cups (330g) caster (superfine) sugar
½ cup (125ml) lime juice
¼ cup (60ml) lemon juice
1 tablespoon finely grated lime rind
green food colouring
blood orange butter
4 eggs, beaten lightly, strained
185g (6 ounces) unsalted butter, chopped
¾ cup (165g) caster (superfine) sugar
1 cup (250ml) blood orange juice
1 tablespoon finely grated blood orange rind

1 For passionfruit butter, combine ingredients
in medium heatproof bowl over medium saucepan
of simmering water. Stir until mixture thickly
coats back of a wooden spoon. Remove from heat.
2 Stand bowl in sink of cold water, stirring
occasionally, about 10 minutes. Pour into hot
sterilised jars; seal.
3 For lime butter, combine ingredients, except rind
and colouring, in medium heatproof bowl; cook as
per passionfruit butter. Stir in rind and colouring
before pouring into sterilised jars.
4 For blood orange butter, combine ingredients,
except rind, in medium heatproof bowl; cook as per
passionfruit butter. Stir in rind before pouring into
sterilised jars.

prep + cook time 1 hour 15 minutes (+ cooling)
makes 3 cups each
tip Will keep for up to four weeks in refrigerator.

fruit butters

spicy mustard pickles

This is an old-fashioned pickle that is splendid with cold roast lamb or cheddar cheese. For a delicious snack, mix it with grated cheese, pile it on toast and grill.

fig and quince paste

spicy mustard pickles

¼ medium cauliflower (400g),
    chopped coarsely
250g (8 ounces) green beans, trimmed,
    chopped coarsely
3 medium brown onions (450g), sliced thickly
1 medium red capsicum (bell pepper) (200g),
    sliced thickly
¼ cup (70g) coarse cooking salt (kosher salt)
2 teaspoons dry mustard
2 tablespoons wholegrain mustard
3 teaspoons curry powder
¼ teaspoon ground turmeric
2 cups (500ml) white vinegar
1 cup (220g) firmly packed light brown sugar
2 tablespoons plain (all-purpose) flour

1 Combine vegetables and salt in large bowl.
Cover; stand overnight.
2 Rinse vegetables; drain. Stir vegetables,
mustards, curry powder, turmeric, 1¾ cups of the
vinegar and sugar in large saucepan over heat,
without boiling, until sugar dissolves; bring to
the boil. Reduce heat; simmer, uncovered, about
10 minutes or until vegetables are just tender.
3 Stir in blended flour and remaining
vinegar; stir over heat until mixture boils and
thickens. Pour into hot sterilised jars; seal.

prep + cook time 50 mins (+ standing)
makes 4 cups

fig and quince paste

1kg (2 pounds) quinces
1 cup (190g) coarsely chopped dried figs
1 cinnamon stick
4 cups (880g) caster (superfine) sugar,
    approximately
¼ cup (60ml) lemon juice

1 Peel, core and quarter quinces. Combine
in large saucepan with figs, cinnamon
and enough water to cover; bring to the boil.
Simmer, covered, about 1 hour or until
most liquid is absorbed. Discard cinnamon;
process mixture until pulpy.
2 Measure mixture into same cleaned pan.
Add 1 cup sugar to every 1 cup pulp; stir in
juice. Stir over low heat until sugar dissolves.
Cook, over very low heat, about 2 hours or until
mixture leaves side of pan.
3 Pour mixture into oiled and lined deep
20cm (8-inch) round cake pan. Stand at room
temperature overnight until set.

prep + cook time 3½ hours (+ standing)
makes 4 cups

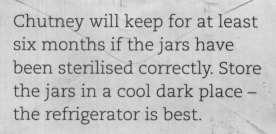

green mango chutney

6 medium green mangoes (2kg), peeled, chopped coarsely
1 tablespoon coarse cooking salt (kosher salt)
1¾ cups (385g) white (granulated) sugar
2½ cups (625ml) brown vinegar
8cm piece fresh ginger (40g), grated
2 cloves garlic, crushed
¾ cup (110g) coarsely chopped dried dates
¾ cup (120g) coarsely chopped raisins
1 teaspoon each chilli powder, ground cinnamon and ground cumin

1 Place mango and salt in large bowl; barely cover with cold water. Cover; stand overnight.
2 Drain mango; discard water. Stir sugar and vinegar in large saucepan over heat, without boiling, until sugar dissolves. Stir in mango and remaining ingredients; simmer, uncovered, stirring occasionally, about 45 minutes or until mixture is thick. Pour into hot sterilised jars; seal.

prep + cook time 1 hour 25 minutes (+ standing)
makes 8 cups

peach chutney

7 large peaches (1.5kg)
1 large brown onion (200g), chopped finely
¾ cup (120g) coarsely chopped raisins
1½ cups (330g) firmly packed light brown sugar
¾ cup (180ml) cider vinegar
1 cinnamon stick
4 cardamom pods, bruised
1 teaspoon whole allspice
2 teaspoons finely grated lemon rind

1 Cut small cross in bottom of each peach. Lower peaches gently into large saucepan of boiling water; boil 1 minute, then place in large bowl of cold water. Peel peaches, discard stones, then chop coarsely.
2 Combine peaches with remaining ingredients in large saucepan; stir over low heat until sugar dissolves. Bring to the boil. Reduce heat; simmer, uncovered, stirring occasionally, about 45 minutes or until thick.
3 Pour chutney into hot sterilised jars; seal immediately.

prep + cook time 1 hour 10 minutes
makes 8 cups

Green mango chutney is a classic condiment to serve with curries and is also excellent with cold meats.

peach chutney

green mango chutney

Store tomato pasta sauce in a cool dark place for up to 12 months; no need to refrigerate. This sauce is delicious heated and served over cooked pasta or used as a base in bolognese sauce, lasagnes and soups. It is best to use either 2-cup (500ml) jars (serves 4) or 3-cup (750ml) jars (serves 6).

traditional italian tomato pasta sauce

10kg (20 pounds) ripe egg tomatoes
18 fresh basil leaves

1 Trim tops from tomatoes; cut tomatoes in half lengthways. Scrape seeds from tomato halves.
2 Place tomato halves in two large saucepans; cook, covered, over low heat, stirring occasionally, about 30 minutes or until tomatoes begin to soften. Remove from heat; cool 10 minutes. Using a large jug, carefully skim excess water from the top of each pan (approximately 1½ cups from each pan).
3 Blend or process tomatoes, in batches, until smooth. Push tomato puree through fine sieve, in batches, into large bowl or jug; discard solids.
4 Pour tomato puree into sterilised jars or bottles; push three basil leaves into each bottle. Seal.
5 Wrap bottles in tea towels or layers of newspaper; pack upright bottles tightly into base of large tall saucepan. Cover bottles with boiling water; bring to the boil. Boil for 1 hour, replenishing water to maintain level. Cool bottles in water.

prep + cook time 5 hours (+ cooling)
makes 5.5 litres

We used very ripe egg tomatoes. You will find specially grown sauce tomatoes at your local markets in the late summer months. Try frying a finely chopped small onion in a medium saucepan; add the sauce. Simmer, uncovered, about 15 minutes or until sauce is thick and a rich red colour. Stir in a handful of frozen peas and season to taste. Toss through cooked penne pasta for a classic Sicilian dish. If you're making sauce to sell, you could type these reheating instructions, and print labels or swing tags to attach to jars.

apple jelly

apple jelly

5 medium green apples (750g), chopped coarsely
1½ litres (6 cups) water
4 cups (880g) white (granulated) sugar,
    approximately

1 Place apples (seeds, skin, cores and all)
and the water in large saucepan; bring to the
boil. Simmer, covered, 1 hour. Strain mixture
through fine cloth; discard pulp.
2 Measure apple liquid; allow 1 cup of sugar
for each cup of liquid.
3 Place apple liquid and sugar in large
saucepan; stir over heat, without boiling,
until sugar dissolves. Bring to the boil; boil,
uncovered, 15 minutes or until jelly sets.
4 Pour into hot sterilised jars; seal immediately.

prep + cook time 1 hour 25 minutes
makes 3 cups

dark plum jam

28 medium blood plums (2kg)
1 litre (4 cups) water
⅓ cup (80ml) lemon juice
1.3kg (6 cups) white (granulated) sugar

1 Cut plums into quarters; discard stones.
Place plums and the water in large saucepan;
bring to the boil. Reduce heat; simmer,
covered, 1 hour.
2 Add juice and sugar; stir over heat, without
boiling, until sugar dissolves. Boil, uncovered,
without stirring, 20 minutes or until jam gels
when tested.
3 Pour into hot sterilised jars; seal immediately.

prep + cook time 1 hour 45 minutes (+ cooling)
makes 8 cups

dark plum jam

Harissa is extremely hot. Serve in small amounts with meat, poultry and couscous, if desired. Harissa will keep in the fridge for up to 10 days. Large, dried chillies are available from Asian food stores.

spicy chilli paste (harissa)

45g (1½ ounces) dried long red chillies
2 teaspoons each cumin seeds and
    coriander seeds
100g (3½ ounces) roasted red capsicum
    (bell pepper), chopped coarsely
3 cloves garlic, crushed
2 teaspoons sea salt
¼ cup (60ml) extra virgin olive oil
extra virgin olive oil, extra

1 Trim and discard chilli stems; place chillies in small heatproof bowl. Cover with boiling water; stand 1 hour. Drain.
2 Meanwhile, dry-fry cumin and coriander seeds in small frying pan until fragrant. Cool. Use mortar and pestle to coarsely crush seeds.
3 Process chillies until chopped finely. Add the crushed seeds, capsicum, garlic, salt, oil and ¼ cup water; process until mixture forms a thick paste.
4 Spoon the mixture into small sterilised jars. Drizzle extra oil over surface; secure lids. Refrigerate.

prep + cook time 25 minutes (+ standing)
makes 2½ cups

spicy chilli paste (harissa)

Serve mushrooms with crusty bread or as part of an antipasto platter with cheeses and deli meats.

marinated mushrooms

1 litre (4 cups) white vinegar
1 cup (250ml) dry white wine
1 tablespoon sea salt flakes
800g (1½ pounds) button mushrooms, halved
2 cloves garlic, sliced thinly
½ teaspoon dried chilli flakes
1 tablespoon coarsely chopped fresh rosemary
1 tablespoon finely chopped fresh
   flat-leaf parsley
3 x 5cm (2-inch) strips lemon rind
1 bay leaf
2 cups (500ml) olive oil

1 Sterilise 1-litre (4-cup) jar and lid.
2 Combine vinegar, wine and half the salt in medium saucepan; heat without boiling. Add mushrooms; simmer, uncovered, about 5 minutes or until tender. Drain mushrooms; discard liquid.
3 Combine hot mushrooms, garlic, chilli, herbs, rind, bay leaf and remaining salt in large heatproof bowl. Spoon mushroom mixture into hot sterilised jar.
4 Heat oil in small saucepan; carefully pour over mushrooms to completely cover mushrooms, leaving a 1cm (½-inch) space between mushrooms and top of jar. Seal while hot.

prep + cook time 40 minutes **makes** 4 cups
tips Store marinated mushrooms in refrigerator for up to three months.

marinated mushrooms

quince jelly

6 medium quinces (2kg)
1.75 litres (7 cups) water
5 cups (1.1kg) white (granulated) sugar,
   approximately
½ cup (125ml) lemon juice, strained

1 Chop unpeeled, uncored quinces coarsely.
Combine quince and the water in large
saucepan; bring to the boil. Reduce heat;
simmer, covered, about 1 hour or until quince
is soft.
2 Strain mixture through fine cloth; stand
overnight. Allow liquid to drip through cloth
slowly; do not squeeze cloth. Discard pulp.
3 Measure quince liquid; allow one cup of
sugar for each cup of quince liquid.

4 Combine quince liquid and sugar in large
saucepan; stir over low heat until sugar
dissolves. Stir in juice; bring to the boil. Boil,
uncovered, without stirring, about 25 minutes
or until jelly sets when tested on a cold saucer.
5 Pour jelly into hot sterilised jars; seal
while hot.

prep + cook time 1 hour 35 minutes
(+ standing) **makes** about 5 cups
tip Store jelly in a cool, dark place for up to
12 months. Refrigerate jelly once opened.

marinated capsicums

3 medium red capsicums (bell peppers) (600g)
3 medium yellow capsicums (bell peppers) (600g)
1 litre (4 cups) white vinegar
2 cups (500ml) water
2 teaspoons salt
1 clove garlic, sliced finely
½ teaspoon dried thyme
3 dried bay leaves
½ teaspoon cracked black pepper
1½ cups (375ml) hot olive oil, approximately

1 Remove seeds and membranes from
capsicums; cut capsicums into 4cm (1½-inch)
strips. Heat vinegar, the water and salt in
non-reactive pan until hot; do not boil. Add
capsicum; simmer gently, uncovered, for
15 minutes; drain. Discard vinegar mixture.
2 Combine hot capsicum, garlic, thyme, bay
leaves and pepper in large heatproof bowl.
Add hot oil, taking care, as it will bubble. Place
capsicum mixture in sterilised 1 litre (4-cup)
jar; top with enough oil to cover capsicum,
leaving 1cm (½-inch) space between capsicum
and top of jar. Seal while hot.

prep + cook time 40 minutes
makes 4 cups

Marinated capsicums can be stored in the refrigerator for up to three months.

7

marinated capsicums

Orange & Poppyseed Macaroon $3.50

SPECIAL
All biscuit packs
3 for
$21·00
or 8·00 each

spiced fig and apple jam

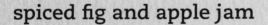

This tart-sweet chutney is a perfect partner to hot or cold poultry and pork.

spiced fig and apple jam

2 large granny smith apples (500g), peeled,
  cored, chopped finely
2 cups (500ml) water
16 medium fresh figs (1 kg), chopped coarsely
½ cup (125ml) orange juice
1.1kg (5 cups) caster (superfine) sugar,
  approximately
2 tablespoons finely grated orange rind
3 star anise
1 cinnamon stick, halved
2 vanilla beans, halved lengthways

1 Combine apple and the water in large
saucepan; bring to the boil. Reduce heat;
simmer, covered, about 20 minutes or
until apple is soft. Add figs and juice;
simmer, covered, 10 minutes.
2 Measure fruit mixture; allow ¾ cup (165g)
sugar for each cup of mixture. Return mixture
and sugar to pan with remaining ingredients;
stir over heat, without boiling, until sugar
dissolves. Boil, uncovered, about 45 minutes
or until jam gels when tested.
3 Pour into hot sterilised jars; seal immediately.

prep + cook time 1½ hours **makes** 8 cups
tip Finely grate the rind from the oranges
before juicing them.

rhubarb chutney

1kg (2 pounds) rhubarb, chopped coarsely
2 medium brown onions (300g),
  chopped coarsely
3 cups (660g) firmly packed light brown sugar
1½ cups (240g) sultanas
2½ cups (625ml) white vinegar
1 tablespoon mustard seeds
1 teaspoon each mixed spice and
  ground ginger

1 Combine ingredients in large saucepan; bring
to the boil. Reduce heat; simmer, uncovered,
stirring occasionally, about 1¼ hours or until
mixture thickens.
2 Pour into hot sterilised jars; seal immediately.

prep + cook time 1½ hours **makes** 5 cups

The marmalade will keep, unopened, for six months in a cool dry place out of direct sunlight. Once opened, it can be refrigerated for up to three months.

pink grapefruit marmalade

6 medium pink or red grapefruit (1.75kg), unpeeled, scrubbed
2 litres (8 cups) water
4½ cups (1kg) white (granulated) sugar

1 Cut thin slices from the ends of each grapefruit and discard. Use vegetable peeler to peel the rind thinly from the grapefruit. Using a sharp knife, discard any white pith from the rind and thinly slice the rind. Use a sharp knife to remove the white pith from the grapefruit; discard the pith. Roughly chop the grapefruit.
2 Place grapefruit and rind in large heavy-based saucepan with the water. Cover; bring to the boil. Remove lid; reduce heat. Simmer, uncovered, about 1½ hours, stirring occasionally, or until grapefruit rind is very soft and mixture is reduced by about half.
3 Meanwhile, preheat oven to 120°C/250°F. Place sugar in shallow ovenproof dish; warm for 15 minutes.

4 Add the warm sugar to the grapefruit mixture; stir over low heat, without boiling, until sugar dissolves. Bring to the boil; boil, uncovered, without stirring, about 15 minutes or until marmalade gels when tested.
5 Remove from heat; skim any scum from surface. Stand marmalade for 15 minutes (this will help to suspend the rind through the mixture). Pour the hot marmalade into hot, sterilised jars. Seal while hot; invert jars onto lids until cool.

prep + cook time 2 hours 30 minutes (+ standing & cooling) **makes** 6 cups

pink grapefruit marmalade

sweet chilli sauce

sweet chilli sauce

250g (8 ounces) fresh long red chillies
3 cups (750ml) white vinegar
2 cups (500ml) water
2 cups (440g) white (granulated) sugar
2 teaspoons salt
6 cloves garlic, crushed

1 Remove green stems from chillies; chop chillies coarsely with their seeds. Process chilli until finely chopped.
2 Combine vinegar, the water, sugar and salt in large saucepan. Stir over low heat, without boiling, until sugar dissolves. Add chilli; boil, uncovered, 20 minutes.
3 Add garlic; boil, uncovered, about 20 minutes or until mixture is reduced to 3 cups (750ml). The sauce will thicken on cooling. Stand sauce 10 minutes.
4 Pour hot sauce into hot sterilised bottles; seal immediately. Cool; refrigerate.

prep + cook time 1 hour 15 minutes
makes 3 cups
tip This recipe can be made two months ahead; store in the refrigerator.

whisky seville marmalade

4 medium seville oranges (1kg)
2 litres (8 cups) water
2.4kg (11 cups) white (granulated) sugar, approximately
¼ cup (60ml) whisky

1 Slice unpeeled oranges thinly; reserve seeds.
2 Put seeds and 1 cup (250ml) of the water in small bowl; cover, set aside. Place sliced fruit in large bowl with remaining water. Stand both fruit mixture and seeds, separately, overnight.
3 Drain seeds over small bowl; reserve liquid. Discard seeds. Combine fruit mixture and seed liquid in large saucepan; bring to the boil. Reduce heat; simmer, covered, about 1 hour or until rind is tender.
4 Measure fruit mixture; allow 1 cup sugar to each cup of fruit mixture. Return fruit mixture with sugar to pan; stir over heat, without boiling, until sugar dissolves. Boil, uncovered, stirring occasionally, about 30 minutes or until marmalade gels when tested. Stand 5 minutes; stir in whisky. Pour hot marmalade into hot sterilised jars; seal immediately.

prep + cook time 2 hours (+ standing)
makes 10 cups

$5

$7

whisky seville marmalade

sweet orange marmalade

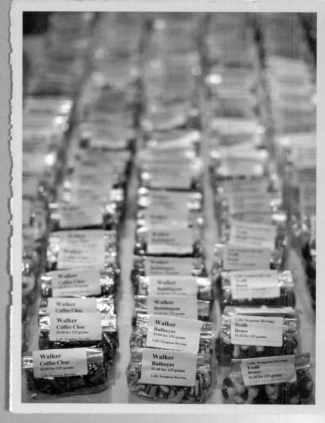

strawberry conserve

sweet orange marmalade

5 large oranges (1.5kg)
1.25 litres (5 cups) water
2 teaspoons citric acid
2 tablespoons lemon juice
5 cups (1.1kg) white (granulated) sugar

1 Cut oranges into quarters. Using sharp knife, remove pith and rind from each quarter. Reserve half the pith; discard the rest. Cut orange flesh into thin slices; place in large bowl, reserve seeds. Cut rind into very thin strips; place in bowl with orange flesh. Add half of the water, cover; stand overnight.
2 Tie reserved seeds and pith in piece of muslin; place bag into separate bowl with citric acid and the remaining water. Cover; stand overnight.
3 Combine contents of bowls with juice in large saucepan; bring to the boil. Reduce heat; simmer, covered, about 40 minutes or until rind is soft. Discard muslin bag.
4 Add sugar; stir over heat, without boiling, until sugar dissolves. Bring to the boil; boil, uncovered, without stirring, about 15 minutes or until marmalade gels when tested. Stand 10 minutes. Pour into hot sterilised jars; seal immediately.

prep + cook time 1 hour 25 minutes (+ standing)
makes 7 cups

The seeds and pith are reserved because they contain high levels of pectin, which will help the marmalade to set.

The way to test whether a jam is set is to put a spoonful of it onto a freezer-chilled saucer. Push the jam with your finger; if it wrinkles, the jam is set. If it doesn't wrinkle, cook for a little longer, then test again.

strawberry conserve

1.5kg (3 pounds) strawberries, hulled
1.1kg (5 cups) white (granulated) sugar
1 cup (250ml) lemon juice

1 Gently heat berries in large saucepan, covered, 5 minutes to extract juice from berries. Transfer berries with slotted spoon to large bowl; reserve.
2 Add sugar and lemon juice to strawberry juice in pan; stir over heat, without boiling, until sugar dissolves. Bring to the boil; boil, uncovered, without stirring, 20 minutes. Return reserved berries to pan; simmer, uncovered, without stirring, 25 minutes or until jam gels when tested.
3 Pour hot jam into hot sterilised jars; seal immediately.

prep + cook time 1 hour 10 mins (+ cooling)
makes 6 cups
tip You will need about three medium lemons (420g) to get the amount of juice required. The lemon adds pectin to help the jam set.

chilli jam

Chilli jam is really hot and you will find a little goes a long way. If you want to decrease the heat dramatically, remove the seeds from the chillies – use disposable gloves to do this. The jam is best poured into small jars; it will keep indefinitely if the jars have been sterilised correctly. Store the jam in a cool dark place. Once opened, store it in the refrigerator.

chilli jam

750g (1½ pounds) fresh long red chillies, chopped coarsely
vegetable oil, for deep-frying
3 large brown onions (600g), chopped coarsely
16 shallots (400g), chopped coarsely
10 cloves garlic, peeled, chopped coarsely
10cm (4-inch) piece fresh ginger (50g), peeled, chopped coarsely
1 cup (200g) coarsely chopped palm sugar
¼ cup (85g) tamarind pulp
⅓ cup (80ml) fish sauce

1 Deep-fry chilli, in batches, in hot oil until soft; drain on absorbent paper. Reheat oil; deep-fry combined onion, shallot, garlic and ginger, in batches, until browned lightly. Drain on absorbent paper.
2 Combine vegetables with 1 cup (250ml) of the cooking oil in large bowl. Process, in batches, until almost smooth.
3 Cook chilli mixture in large heavy-based saucepan over low heat, stirring, for about 10 minutes. Add sugar; cook, stirring, 10 minutes. Add remaining ingredients; cook over low heat, stirring occasionally, about 2 hours or until thick and dark red in colour.
4 Pour jam into hot sterilised jars; seal the jars immediately.

prep + cook time 3 hours **makes** 6 cups

tomato chutney

preserved lemons

10 medium lemons (1.4kg)
¾ cup (165g) coarse cooking salt (kosher salt)
8 whole cloves
4 cardamom pods, bruised
½ teaspoon coriander seeds
4 bay leaves
2 cups (500ml) lemon juice, approximately

1 Wash and dry lemons; cut into quarters lengthways. Place lemons in large bowl; sprinkle evenly with salt.
2 Pack lemons in sterilised jars with spices and bay leaves.
3 Pour over enough juice to cover the lemons completely; secure lids. Stand in a cool dry place for at least three weeks before using.

prep + cook time 10 minutes (+ 3 weeks standing) **makes** 6 cups

tomato chutney

10 medium ripe tomatoes (1.5kg), peeled, chopped coarsely
2 large apples (400g), peeled, chopped coarsely
2 medium brown onions (300g), chopped coarsely
1 cup (220g) firmly packed light brown sugar
1½ cups (375ml) brown vinegar
¼ teaspoon chilli powder
½ teaspoon dry mustard
¾ cup (120g) sultanas
1 clove garlic, crushed
2 teaspoons each curry powder and ground allspice

1 Stir ingredients in large saucepan over heat, without boiling, until sugar dissolves; bring to the boil. Reduce heat; simmer, uncovered, stirring occasionally, about 1 hour or until mixture is thick.
2 Pour chutney into hot sterilised jars; seal immediately.

prep + cook time 1 hour 30 mins
makes 6 cups
tips Tomato chutney makes a great addition to casseroles, rissoles, burgers and pot roasts.

preserved lemons

To use, remove and discard the flesh from the lemons. Chop or slice the rind and use in tagines or dips, with lamb dishes or sprinkled over fish. This recipe is best made a month ahead. Refrigerate the preserved lemons after opening.

dukkah

dukkah

⅔ cup (110g) blanched almonds
⅔ cup (110g) hazelnuts
½ cup (75g) sesame seeds
¼ cup (20g) coriander seeds
2 tablespoons cumin seeds
2 teaspoons freshly ground black pepper
2 teaspoons flaked sea salt

1 Preheat oven to 180°C/350°F.
2 Spread nuts separately, in single layers, on oven trays. Roast about 10 minutes or until browned lightly and fragrant. Transfer hazelnuts to clean tea towel; rub nuts to remove as much of the skin as possible. Cool.
3 Meanwhile, dry-fry sesame seeds in medium frying pan over low heat, stirring occasionally, until browned lightly. Transfer sesame seeds to large heatproof bowl; cool.
4 Process almonds and hazelnuts until chopped finely; add to sesame seeds.
5 Dry-fry coriander and cumin seeds in same medium frying pan, over low heat, stirring occasionally, until fragrant; cool. Grind seeds using a mortar and pestle.
6 Add seeds to almond mixture with pepper and salt; mix well. Store in airtight jars.

prep + cook time 40 minutes
makes about 2½ cups

dukkah

Dukkah is delicious with olive oil and bread, or sprinkled over salads, vegetables, barbecued meat, seafood and soups. Store in an airtight container for up to one month.

glossary

ALLSPICE also called pimento or jamaican pepper; tastes like a combination of nutmeg, cumin, clove and cinnamon. Available whole or ground.

ALMONDS flat, pointed ended nuts with pitted brown shell enclosing a creamy white kernel which is covered by a brown skin.
blanched brown skins removed.
essence often interchangeable with extract; made with almond oil and alcohol or another agent.
flaked paper-thin slices.
ground also known as almond meal; nuts are powdered to a coarse flour texture.
marzipan made from ground almonds, sugar and glucose. Similar to almond paste but is not as strong in flavour but is finer in consistency and more pliable. We refer to this as ready made almond icing.
paste a combination of ground almonds or almond meal, sugar and egg or glucose which is used as a cake icing.Generally has a stronger flavour than marzipan but is not as pliable.
slivered small pieces cut lengthways.
vienna toffee-coated almonds.

BAKING PAPER also known as parchment paper or baking parchment – is a silicone-coated paper that is primarily used for lining baking pans and oven trays so cakes and biscuits won't stick.

BAKING POWDER a raising agent consisting mainly of two parts cream of tartar to one part bicarbonate of soda.

BICARBONATE OF SODA raising agent also known as baking soda.

BUTTER we use salted butter unless stated otherwise; 125g is equal to 1 stick (4 ounces).

CACHOUS also called dragées in some countries; minuscule metallic-looking-but-edible confectionery balls used in cake decorating.

CAPSICUM also called pepper or bell pepper. Discard seeds and membranes before use.

CARDAMOM a spice native to India and used extensively in its cuisine; can be purchased in pod, seed or ground form.

CHEESE
cheddar the most common cow milk 'tasty' cheese; should be aged, hard and have a pronounced bite. For our lower-fat versions we used one with no more than 20% fat.

cream commonly known as Philadelphia or Philly, a soft cow milk cheese with a fat content of at least 33%. Sold at supermarkets in bulk and packaged.

CHILLI use rubber gloves when seeding and chopping fresh chillies as they can burn your skin. We use unseeded chillies because the seeds contain the heat; use fewer chillies rather than seeding the lot.
flakes also sold as crushed chilli; dehydrated deep-red, extremely fine slices and whole seeds.
long red available both fresh and dried; a generic term used for any moderately hot, long, thin chilli (about 6cm to 8cm long).
powder the Asian variety is the hottest, made from dried ground Thai chillies; can be used instead of fresh in the proportion of ½ teaspoon chilli powder to 1 medium chopped fresh red chilli.

CHOCOLATE
choc bits also known as chocolate chips or chocolate morsels; available in milk, white and dark chocolate. Made of cocoa liquor, cocoa butter, sugar and an emulsifier, these hold their shape in baking and are ideal for decorating.
dark cooking also called compounded chocolate; good for cooking as it doesn't require tempering and sets at room temperature. Made with vegetable fat instead of cocoa butter so it lacks the rich, buttery flavour of eating chocolate. Cocoa butter is the most expensive component in chocolate, so the substitution of a vegetable fat means that compounded chocolate is much cheaper to produce.
dark eating also known as semi-sweet or luxury chocolate; made of a high percentage of cocoa liquor and cocoa butter, and little added sugar. Unless stated otherwise, we use dark eating chocolate in this book as it's ideal for use in desserts and cakes.
hazelnut spread We use Nutella. Created when chocolate was in short supply during World War 2, so hazelnuts were added to the chocolate to increase supply.
melts small discs of compounded milk, white or dark chocolate ideal for melting and moulding.
milk most popular eating chocolate, mild and very sweet; similar in make-up to dark with the difference being the addition of milk solids.
white contains no cocoa solids but derives its sweet flavour from cocoa butter. Very sensitive to heat.

COARSE COOKING SALT also known as kosher salt, coarser grained than table salt and used for pickles and preserves.

COCO POPS chocolate-flavoured puffed rice.

COCOA POWDER also known as unsweetened cocoa; cocoa beans (cacao seeds) that have been fermented, roasted, shelled, ground into powder then cleared of most of the fat content.

COCONUT
desiccated concentrated, dried, unsweetened and finely shredded coconut flesh.
extract synthetically produced from flavouring, oil and alcohol.
flaked dried flaked coconut flesh.
shredded unsweetened strips of dried coconut flesh.

CORN FLAKES commercially manufactured cereal made of dehydrated then baked crisp flakes of corn.

CORNFLOUR also known as cornstarch. Available made from corn or wheat (wheaten cornflour gives a lighter texture in cakes); used as a thickening agent.

CREAM we used fresh cream, also known as pure or pouring cream unless otherwise stated. Has no additives. Minimum fat content 35%.
thick (double) a dolloping cream with a minimum fat content of 45%.
thickened (heavy) a whipping cream containing thickener. Minimum fat content 35%.
sour a thick commercially cultured soured cream. Minimum fat content 35%.

CUSTARD POWDER instant mixture used to make pouring custard; similar to North American instant pudding mixes.

EGGS we use large chicken eggs weighing an average of 60g unless stated otherwise in the recipes in this book. If a recipe calls for raw or barely cooked eggs, exercise caution if there is a salmonella problem in your area, particularly in food eaten by children and pregnant women.

FLOUR
plain also known as all-purpose; unbleached wheat flour is the best for baking: the gluten content ensures a strong dough and produces a light result.
rice very fine, almost powdery, gluten-free flour; made from ground white rice. Used in baking, as a thickener, and in some Asian noodles and desserts.
self-raising all-purpose plain or wholemeal flour with baking powder and salt added; make it yourself with plain or wholemeal flour sifted with baking powder in the proportion of 1 cup flour to 2 teaspoons baking powder.

wholemeal also known as wholewheat flour; milled with the wheat germ so is higher in fibre and more nutritional than plain flour.

FOOD COLOURING edible dyes that can be used to change the colour of various foods, without noticeably changing the taste.

GELATINE we use dried (powdered) gelatine in this book; it's also available in sheet form known as leaf gelatine. A thickening agent made from either collagen, a protein found in animal connective tissue and bones, or certain algae (agar-agar). Three teaspoons of dried gelatine (8g or one sachet) is about the same as four gelatine leaves. The two types are interchangable but leaf gelatine gives a much clearer mixture than dried gelatine; it's perfect in dishes where appearance matters.

GINGER
fresh also called green or root ginger; the thick gnarled root of a tropical plant. Can be kept, peeled, covered with dry sherry in a jar and refrigerated, or frozen in an airtight container.
glacé fresh ginger root preserved in sugar syrup; crystallised ginger (sweetened with cane sugar) can be substituted if rinsed with warm water and dried before using.
ground also called powdered ginger; used as a flavouring in baking but cannot be substituted for fresh ginger.

GLACE FRUIT fruit such as peaches, pineapple and orange cooked in heavy sugar syrup then dried.

GLUCOSE SYRUP also known as liquid glucose, made from wheat starch; used in jam and confectionery making. Available at health-food stores and supermarkets.

GOLDEN SYRUP a by-product of refined sugarcane; pure maple syrup or honey can be substituted. Treacle is similar, but more viscous, and has a stronger flavour and aroma than golden syrup.

HONEY the variety sold in a squeezable container is not suitable for the recipes in this book.

HUNDREDS AND THOUSANDS tiny sugar-syrup-coated sugar crystal balls that come in a variety of colours for cake decorating.

JELLY CRYSTALS a combination of sugar, gelatine, colours and flavours; when dissolved in water, the solution sets as firm jelly.

glossary

MAPLE SYRUP distilled from the sap of sugar maple trees found only in Canada and the USA. Most often eaten with pancakes or waffles, but also used as an ingredient in baking or in preparing desserts. Maple-flavoured syrup or pancake syrup is not an adequate substitute for the real thing.

MILK we use full-cream homogenised milk unless otherwise specified.
buttermilk in spite of its name, buttermilk is actually low in fat, varying between 0.6 per cent and 2.0 per cent per 100ml. Originally the term given to the slightly sour liquid left after butter was churned from cream, today it is intentionally made from no-fat or low-fat milk to which specific bacterial cultures have been added.
evaporated unsweetened canned milk from which water has been extracted by evaporation.
sweetened condensed a canned milk product consisting of milk with more than half the water content removed and sugar added.

MIXED PEEL candied citrus peel.

MUSCATELS dried muscat grapes; distinctively musty flavour goes well with cheese and chocolate.

ORANGES
blood a virtually seedless citrus fruit with blood-red-streaked rind and flesh; sweet, non-acidic, salmon-coloured pulp and juice with slight strawberry or raspberry overtones.
seville very tart; suitable only for jam-making.

PEANUT BUTTER peanuts ground to a paste; available in crunchy and smooth varieties.

POPPING CORN a variety of dried corn that is sold as kernels for popcorn

POPPY SEEDS small, dried, bluish-grey seeds of the poppy plant, with a crunchy texture and a nutty flavour. Can be purchased whole or ground.

QUINCE yellow-skinned fruit with hard texture and astringent, tart taste; eaten cooked or as a preserve.

READY-MADE WHITE ICING also known as soft icing, ready-to-roll and prepared fondant.

ROLLED OATS flattened oat grain rolled into flakes and traditionally used for porridge. Instant oats are also available, but use traditional oats for baking.

ROSEWATER extract made from crushed rose petals; used for its aromatic quality in desserts.

SUGAR we use coarse, granulated white table sugar, also known as crystal sugar, unless the recipe specifies otherwise.
brown a soft, finely granulated sugar retaining molasses for its characteristic colour and flavour.
caster also known as superfine or finely granulated table sugar.
demerara small-grained, golden crystal sugar.
icing also known as confectioners' sugar or powdered sugar; pulverised granulated sugar crushed together with a small amount of cornflour.
palm also called nam tan pip, jaggery, jawa or gula melaka; made from the sap of the sugar palm tree; substitute with brown sugar if it is unavailable.

STAR ANISE a dried star-shaped pod whose seeds have an astringent aniseed flavour; commonly used to flavour stocks and marinades.

TAMARIND the tamarind tree produces clusters of hairy brown pods, each of which is filled with seeds and a viscous pulp, that are dried and pressed into blocks or soaked in water to make a puree, which is sold in jars. Gives a sweet-sour, slightly astringent taste to marinades, pastes, sauces and dressings.

TREACLE a concentrated, refined sugar syrup with a strong flavour and dark black colour.

VANILLA
bean dried, long, thin pod from a tropical golden orchid; the minuscule black seeds inside the bean are used to impart a luscious vanilla flavour in baking and desserts. Place a whole bean in a jar of sugar to make the vanilla sugar often called for in recipes; a bean can be used three or four times.
extract obtained from vanilla beans infused in water; a non-alcoholic version of essence.

VINEGAR
brown malt made from fermented malt and beech shavings.
cider a brownish yellow vinegar made from the must of fermented apples.
white made from distilled grain alcohol.

YEAST (dried and fresh), a raising agent used in dough and bread making. Granular (7g sachets) and fresh compressed (20g blocks) yeast can almost always be substituted one for the other when yeast is called for.

conversion chart

MEASURES

One Australian metric measuring cup holds approximately 250ml; one Australian metric tablespoon holds 20ml; one Australian metric teaspoon holds 5ml.

The difference between one country's measuring cups and another's is within a two- or three-teaspoon variance, and will not affect your cooking results. Cooks in North America, New Zealand and the United Kingdom use a 15ml tablespoon.

All cup and spoon measurements are level. The most accurate way of measuring dry ingredients is to weigh them. When measuring liquids, use a clear glass or plastic jug with the metric markings.

We use large eggs with an average weight of 60g.

DRY MEASURES

METRIC	IMPERIAL
15g	½oz
30g	1oz
60g	2oz
90g	3oz
125g	4oz (¼lb)
155g	5oz
185g	6oz
220g	7oz
250g	8oz (½lb)
280g	9oz
315g	10oz
345g	11oz
375g	12oz (¾lb)
410g	13oz
440g	14oz
470g	15oz
500g	16oz (1lb)
750g	24oz (1½lb)
1kg	32oz (2lb)

LIQUID MEASURES

METRIC	IMPERIAL
30ml	1 fluid oz
60ml	2 fluid oz
100ml	3 fluid oz
125ml	4 fluid oz
150ml	5 fluid oz
190ml	6 fluid oz
250ml	8 fluid oz
300ml	10 fluid oz
500ml	16 fluid oz
600ml	20 fluid oz
1000ml (1 litre)	1¾ pints

LENGTH MEASURES

METRIC	IMPERIAL
3mm	⅛in
6mm	¼in
1cm	½in
2cm	¾in
2.5cm	1in
5cm	2in
6cm	2½in
8cm	3in
10cm	4in
13cm	5in
15cm	6in
18cm	7in
20cm	8in
23cm	9in
25cm	10in
28cm	11in
30cm	12in (1ft)

OVEN TEMPERATURES

The oven temperatures in this book are for conventional ovens; if you have a fan-forced oven, decrease the temperature by 10-20 degrees.

	°C (CELSIUS)	°F (FAHRENHEIT)
Very slow	120	250
Slow	150	300
Moderately slow	160	325
Moderate	180	350
Moderately hot	200	400
Hot	220	425
Very hot	240	475

The imperial measurements used in these recipes are approximate only. Measurements for cake pans are approximate only. Using same-shaped cake pans of a similar size should not affect the outcome of your baking. We measure the inside top of the cake pan to determine sizes.

index

a

almonds
    almond bread 28
    chocolate marzipan 23
    sugar and spice 25
angel gift tag cookies 90
anzac biscuits 141
apples
    apple cinnamon tea loaves 145
    apple jelly 173
    old-fashioned apple pie slice 134
    toffee apples 54
apricot choc-chip muesli bars 81
apricot squares 133

b

banana
    banana bread 130
    banana cake with passionfruit
      icing 158
    banana cupcakes with maple
      cream frosting 76
berry & orange patty cakes 73
blood orange butter 164
blueberry macaroon slice 150
brandied butter cream 47
brandy butter 96
brownies, chocolate raspberry 71
bubble bars, crunchy 63
butter cream 58
buttercake, cut-and-keep 146
butterfly cakes 150
buttery citrus cake 37

c

cakes see also cupcakes
    banana, with passionfruit
      icing 158
    berry & orange patty cakes 73
    boiled chocolate 142
    boiled fruit cake 111
    butterfly 150
    buttery citrus 37
    carrot 45
    carrot cake with lemon cream
      cheese frosting 156
    chocolate and pecan torte 46
    chocolate chiffon 47
    chocolate drambuie fruit 120
    christmas star cakes 119
    citrus patty cakes 73
    coconut ice 74
    cut-and-keep buttercake 146
    dundee 41

grand marnier christmas 115
hummingbird 42
little christmas 106
little gift 106
madeira 146
orange almond victoria
    sponge 38
passionfruit & white chocolate
patty cakes 73
passionfruit buttermilk 16
patty cakes with glacé icing 73
plum and cinnamon 41
raspberry cream sponge 35
rhubarb custard tea cake 154
rich chocolate christmas
    cakes 116
rock 158
strawberry jelly 35
candied citrus slices 37
candied popcorn 56
capsicums, marinated 176
caramel nut chocolates 19
caramels, creamy 74
carrot cake with lemon cream
    cheese frosting 156
carrot cakes 45
cheese and poppy seed biscuits 133
cherry bakewell tarts 137
chilli jam 189
chilli paste, spicy 174
chocolate
    apricot choc-chip muesli bars 81
    boiled chocolate cake 142
    caramel nut chocolates 19
    chewy chocolate slice 63
    choc-vanilla noughts &
      crosses 72
    chocolate and pecan torte 46
    chocolate chiffon 47
    chocolate coconut rough slice 76
    chocolate drambuie fruit
      cake 120
    chocolate freckle slice 79
    chocolate fudge 70
    chocolate marzipan almonds 23
    chocolate raspberry brownies 71
    christmas star 119
    chunky chewy choc-chip
      cookies 68
    crunchy bubble bars 63
    little chocolate christmas
    puddings 111
    panettone 105
    rich chocolate christmas
      cakes 116
    whoopie pies 26
christmas cookies 90

christmas pudding
    boiled 108
    little chocolate christmas
      puddings 111
    mini 112
christmas star cakes 119
christmas wreaths, lemon-
    glazed 103
chutney
    green mango 168
    peach 168
    rhubarb 181
    tomato 190
citrus patty cakes 73
coconut
    coconut & lime glacé icing 73
    coconut ice 64
    coconut ice cakes 74
    coconut ice frosting 74
cranberry and apple fruit mince 86
creamy caramels 74
crunchy bubble bars 63
custard 154

d

date and walnut rolls 145
drinks
    ginger beer 10
    homemade lemonade 10
    lime cordial 11
    raspberry mint cordial 11
dukkah 193
dundee cake 41
dutch ginger and almond slice 130

f

figs
    fig and apple jam, spiced 181
    fig and nut logs 92
    fig and quince paste 167
    fig mince pies 99
frosting
    coconut ice 74
    fudge 60, 142
    lemon cream cheese 45, 156
    maple cream 76
fruit butters 164
fruit cake, boiled 111
fruit mince
    cranberry and apple 86
    slice 152
fudge, chocolate 70
fudge-frosted cupcakes 60
fudge frosting 142

g

ganache 46
   honeyed white chocolate 30
ginger beer 10
gingerbread christmas trees 100
gingerbread men 67
glacé icing 37, 73, 129
grand marnier christmas cake 115
green mango chutney 168

h

harissa 174
honey joys 56
hummingbird cakes 42

i

icing
   chocolate 63, 126
   coconut & lime glacé icing 73
   glacé 37, 129
   lemon 42, 103, 106
   lemon royal 90
   orange glacé 25, 73
   passionfruit 16, 134
   passionfruit glacé 73
   raspberry glacé 35
   royal 67, 100
italian tomato pasta sauce 171

j

jaffa panforte 92
jam
   chilli 189
   dark plum 173
   jam drops 140
   spiced fig and apple 181

l

lamingtons 126
lemon
   lemon cream cheese
      frosting 45, 156
   lemon glaze 137
   lemon-glazed christmas
      wreaths 103
   lemon squares, tangy 138
   preserved lemons 190
lemonade, homemade 10
lime butter 164
lime cordial 11
little christmas cakes 106
little gift cakes 106

m

macaroons, pistachio, white
   chocolate and honey french 30
madeira cake 146
madeleines 138
marmalade
   pink grapefruit 182
   sweet orange 187
   whisky seville 184
marshmallow, passionfruit 81
marshmallow treats 64
mince pies, fig 99
mini christmas puddings 112
monte carlos 137
muesli, tropical toasted 20
mushrooms, marinated 175
mustard pickles, spicy 167

n

neenish and pineapple tarts 129

o

orange almond victoria sponge 38
orange and almond palmiers 25

p

palmiers, orange and almond 25
panettone, chocolate 105
panforte, jaffa 92
passionfruit
   passionfruit and white chocolate
      patty cakes 73
   passionfruit butter 164
   passionfruit buttermilk cake 16
   passionfruit marshmallows 81
patty cakes with glacé icing 73
peach chutney 168
peanut butter cookies 79
pecan, macadamia and walnut
   pies, mini 157
pickles, spicy mustard 167
pink grapefruit marmalade 182
pistachio, white chocolate and
   honey french macaroons 30
pistachio white chocolate brittle 28
plum and cinnamon cake 41
plum jam, dark 173
popcorn, candied 56
preserved lemons 190

q

quince jelly 176

r

raspberry
   raspberry cream sponge 35
   raspberry glacé icing 35
   raspberry mint cordial 11
rhubarb chutney 181
rhubarb custard tea cake 154
rock cakes 158
rocky road christmas trees 95

s

salted caramel truffles 23
sauce, sweet chilli 184
shortbread, traditional 149
spiced honey cream 145
spiced yo-yos with brandy butter 96
spicy chilli paste 174
spicy mustard pickles 167
stained-glass christmas cookies 89
strawberry conserve 187
strawberry jelly cakes 35
sugar and spice almonds 25
sweet chilli sauce 184
sweet orange marmalade 187

t

tangy lemon squares 138
toffee apples 54
toffee-on-a-stick 60
toffees 54
tomato chutney 190
tomato pasta sauce, traditional
   italian 171
torte, chocolate and pecan 46
tropical toasted muesli 20
truffles, salted caramel 23
turkish delight 20

w

walnut praline 47
whisky seville marmalade 184
white chocolate brittle, with
   pistachios 28
white christmas slice 103
whoopie pies
   chocolate 26
   vanilla 26

y

yo-yos, spiced, with brandy
   butter 96

First published in 2011 by ACP Magazines Ltd,
a division of PBL Media Pty Limited
54 Park St, Sydney
GPO Box 4088, Sydney, NSW 2001.
phone (02) 9282 8618; fax (02) 9267 9438
acpbooks@acpmagazines.com.au; www.acpbooks.com.au

ACP BOOKS
General Manager - Christine Whiston
Associate publisher - Seymour Cohen
Editor-in-Chief - Susan Tomnay
Creative Director & Designer - Hieu Chi Nguyen
Food Director - Pamela Clark

Published and Distributed in the United Kingdom by Octopus Publishing Group
Endeavour House
189 Shaftesbury Avenue
London WC2H 8JY
United Kingdom
phone (+44)(0)207 632 5400; fax (+44)(0)207 632 5405
info@octopus-publishing.co.uk;
www.octopusbooks.co.uk

Printed by C&C Offset Printing., China

International foreign language rights, Brian Cearnes, ACP Books bcearnes@acpmagazines.com.au

A catalogue record for this book is available from the British Library.
ISBN 978-1-74245-071-1